Selling
When No One Is
Buying

GROWING PROSPECTS, CLIENTS, AND SALES IN TOUGH ECONOMIC TIMES

Stephan Schiffman
America's #1 Corporate Sales Trainer

BUSINESS
Avon, Massachusetts

Dedication

To those who are held accountable

Published by Adams Business, an imprint of Adams Media,
a division of F+W Media, Inc.
57 Littlefield Street, Avon, MA 02322

ISBN 10: 1-60550-660-5
ISBN 13: 978-1-60550-660-9
Printed in the United States of America

J I H G F E D C B

Library of Congress Cataloging-in-Publication Data
is available from the publisher.

This publication is designed to provide accurate and authoritative information with regard to the subject matter covered. It is sold with the understanding that the publisher is not engaged in rendering legal, accounting, or other professional advice. If legal advice or other expert assistance is required, the services of a competent professional person should be sought.

—From a *Declaration of Principles* jointly adopted by a Committee of the American Bar Association and a Committee of Publishers and Associations

Many of the designations used by manufacturers and sellers to distinguish their products are claimed as trademarks. Where those designations appear in this book and Adams Media was aware of a trademark claim, the designations have been printed with initial capital letters.

This book is available at quantity discounts for bulk purchases.
For information, please call 1-800-289-0963.

Acknowledgments

Writing a book is a lot like life. The best are shepherded along with the help of friends and mentors. And so it is with this book. I would be remiss if I didn't mention them and my gratitude for their help.

I am grateful to my collaborator, Curt Schleier, who has worked with me on my most recent manuscripts. He is, of course, an excellent writer and editor, with several books and hundreds of articles to his credit. He is also an excellent trainer; Curt teaches business writing skills to corporate executives and government executives. He knows how to ask the right questions that force me to hone in on the problems and situations we're discussing at the moment. But most important of all, he is extremely simpatico and a pleasure to work with. I'm proud to call him my friend.

It goes almost without saying that I want to thank my editor at Adams, Peter Archer.

I'd also like to acknowledge my students. Hundreds of them have stayed in touch, sharing their experiences and ideas with me.

Last—but certainly far from least—this is for Anne, Jennifer, and Daniele, whose support and love keep me going.

Contents

Introduction

Allow me to let you in on a secret. When things are going well, your kindergartner can sell. Okay, I exaggerate, but you get my point: when the economy is going gangbusters and everyone is buying everything in sight, well, it doesn't take a lot of finesse to be a sales rep.

But let's take a look at a different scenario. One in which the economy is in a serious downturn. Consumers aren't buying. As a result, corporations aren't buying. Jobs are going away. And the chances are that there are a lot of really good sales folks out there who aren't selling.

The sad truth is that in these circumstances a lot of them give up and give in. No one's buying, so what's the use? The economy becomes the scapegoat for all their failures. But the truth is it doesn't have to be that way, and you know it and I know it.

How do I know you know? Because you've picked up this book and gotten to the fourth paragraph. So you at least suspect that here is a better path—even if you don't where it's located.

I think I do. And I intend to be your GPS.

In many of my books and all of my courses I talk about the fact that there are essentially two types of salespeople: hunters and gatherers, genuine salespeople and order takers. For the next hundred-plus pages, I'm going to assume that you are a hunter, an aggressive, I'm-gonna-get-this-contract sales rep.

How do I know this? Because you've picked up this book and now have gotten to the seventh paragraph. So I will address you accordingly. By that I mean honestly and on the assumption that you get it. I'm going to make some suggestions that will likely be new to you. I'm going to offer some solutions that have probably been drilled into your head since you were in sales kindergarten. And I am going to motivate you to ignore the newspapers, ignore the nightly news, ignore your own stock portfolio, and just go out and sell.

The truth of the matter is that the last of these items is probably the most important. When times are bad, it's easy to get down on yourself. It's easy to say the economy stinks, so there's no point even to go out to make sales calls.

That is, of course, silly. Your sales mentality can't start with where the economy is. If you do that, too often you'll be beaten before you start. The economy is cyclical. Sometimes it's up; sometimes it's down. But in both parts of the cycle, salespeople have to sell.

Jack Welch, the legendary head of GE during the company's heyday, used to tell his managers he wanted them to come in each day as though it was the first day they joined GE. I think that's a great idea.

Do you remember your first day on your job? Your enthusiasm was probably contagious. I'm guessing you saw nothing but new opportunities and big commissions in your future. You have to recall those emotions, because positive attitude generates positive attitude; a bad attitude generates negativity and creates a climate in which selling is virtually impossible. This is the most important thing I can teach you in this book: *Your sales success is all about attitude.*

The truth of the matter is that a crummy economy is in a strange way liberating, freeing you of restraints that curtailed your creativity.

I'll also be talking a little about being more in control of your life. Richard Branson, the genius behind the Virgin brands, asks the top executives of his companies (Virgin Airlines, Virgin Megastores, etc.) to spend one month every six months signing the checks. If they see where all this money is going, they are more likely to be able to control costs.

Well, it's the same thing with your life. You need to spend some time at least once every six months evaluating where you're going and what your goals are. Are you headed in the right direction? Are you seeing the right people? Making the right cold calls?

Of course, I'm not going to tell you everything in this short introduction. I just wanted to whet your appetite. And also I wanted to stress that no matter what the media tells you, it's not necessary to become a victim of an economic downturn. Instead, you can become a sales star.

When the Economy Sags

Let's start with the basics: As I write this, the housing market has come close to drying up. Thousands of families have defaulted on their mortgages. The price of gasoline hit the stratosphere, and while it's come down substantially from its highs that's only because the economy is so bad it has substantially reduced demand.

Meanwhile, the three largest American automobile manufacturers are losing billions of dollars a year because of their inability to design and manufacture cars that people actually want to drive. They're laying off thousands, while many other companies across all sectors of the economy are outsourcing jobs and manufacturing.

And it isn't just an American problem. Did you know that the pollution in China crosses the Pacific Ocean and affects California? That, of course, is a metaphor for how globalization also plays a role in shaping today's economy—and economic crises. The fact is that today if someone sneezes in Beijing, someone in Milwaukee has to wipe his nose. We're living in an age when economic change doesn't stop at national borders. Much of our economy depends on China, India, and other remote countries. And the workers in those countries know their jobs are linked to the U.S. economy.

But if this sounds scary—or at least, overwhelming—let me give you some positive news.

First of all, the economy tends to go in cycles. Everything that's happened today has occurred before. Some of the elements may have been different, but the idea of a down cycle is clearly not new.

When you're reading this we may be in the midst of great prosperity. Or the world, the American, and your personal economy may still be on a slide. But the important thing to remember is that nothing is permanent. Everything changes.

To a lot of people it looks as though we no longer have control over our lives. That's also frightening. It used to be that we had more control over our lives—or at least it seemed that way. If one company couldn't supply your needs, well there was probably another one around that corner that could and would.

But now that corner may be in China or India. So an earthquake there may interrupt your supply line. And then what do you tell your customers?

The good news is that there are ways to overcome the worst that a bad economy can throw at you. Some of the changes are attitudinal. Some require paying attention to details you may have overlooked. Some require additional hours.

But over the next dozen chapters I'm going to show you myriad ways you can boost sales even when everyone else tells you it's hopeless; no one is buying.

I'm anxious to hear from you about this or any other sales-related matter. Feel free to contact me at *www.steveschiffman.com.* I personally check my e-mail and I personally respond to all.

Finally, I keep forgetting if it was Roy Rogers or Gene Autry who sang, "Happy sales to you, until we meet again." What follows is the Steve Schiffman cover version of that classic.

Stephan Schiffman
New York City
May 2009

Chapter 1

Learn the New Buying Environment

You can't sell if you don't know the landscape. That's the most basic thing. If you're going to sell when no one's buying, step one is to figure out why money has dried up. Step two is to see what that means for you. Step three is to do something about it. If you do your homework, you can make the sale. But you've got to leave complacency at the door.

Just last week (my last week, not your last week), I went to a prospect's office to (I thought) close a deal. I went over the proposal with him—call him Frank—in great detail. When we were finished he said (again): "I love it."

Then he added "This is a done deal."

If only he'd stopped right there. But, no, he had to add seven more words: ". . . as soon as I find the money."

What does that mean? Was he going to walk the halls of his office building with a tin can trying to raise the funds he needed? Was he planning to check under the cushions on the couch in the reception area? I have no idea. And I don't think Frank did either. I do believe he sincerely wanted to proceed—and in a more bullish economy he probably would have had the authority and budget to do so. But one outgrowth of a downturn is increased scrutiny of all spending.

In this case, the fact that Frank did not have the money at his disposal likely meant that his boss was unaware of me, hadn't decided to use me yet, or didn't have any money either. As my daughter might say, "Whatever." It doesn't make a difference. Whatever the reason, the process was being delayed. And here's my first piece of wisdom: The longer it takes to make a deal, the less likely that it will take place. The sense of urgency that was there early on just dissipates.

Why am I telling you this story? Frankly, I usually try to keep sales I didn't make on the Q.T. However, I've found I've learned more from my failures than my successes. And I learned a couple of very important lessons here.

Because I'd done a lot of business with Frank before, I don't think I pressed as much as I should have. We always got along really well. He was open to almost every one of my ideas. I could bounce something off him casually, and if he liked it, if it made sense, he bought it. Frank was the decision maker, and I assumed the deal would materialize like magic.

> *In an economic downturn, the paradigm changes—sometimes quite dramatically.*

Even Companies in the Black Are Seeing Red

But things are different when the economy takes a downturn. I made a mistake not being aware of just how much the landscape had changed. My inability to land this sale forced me to recognize and come to grips with this and to alter my methodology accordingly. You, too, have to understand that in an economic downturn, the paradigm changes–sometimes quite dramatically. You can no longer just barge into a client or prospect's office like a bull in a china shop feeling your professional life can go on as usual.

You should be aware, for example, that many companies are finding ways to delay purchases—and I don't mean that in a running-lean-and-mean, let's-trim-the-fat kind of way. When times are bad, they revert to what I call the good-enough mode.

Sales Tactic

Before you stride into a client's office, plop yourself down in a chair, put on a big smile, and start into your pitch, do your research. Find out what kind of shape the company's in. Are their profits growing, shrinking, or stagnating? Are they expanding into new markets? Or pulling back? In sales, information is power. Don't forget that. *Determine the economic landscape you're selling into.*

Consider the story of a friend of mine who created a software program that helps companies dispatch employees—plumbers, electricians, carpenters, etc.—to do repairs. It was superior to anything out there—but not a quantum leap forward. When he went out to sell it, almost all the people he showed it to liked what they saw. But at the same time, they all said money was a little tight and what they had now was good enough.

Consider the manufacturers of computers. Many large IT departments are delaying their normal replacement cycle because the PCs they currently have are good enough for their present needs. For example, since the company is using less product, the cycle is that much longer. I am working with a company now that buys ball bearings, and they seem to have found that the supplies the people are using are lasting longer. Of course, the reason is that they are not manufacturing at the same rate! Hence, they need less.

Well, you might say, of course industries faced with hardships will make cutbacks—whether the global economy is bad or good. I agree. But when times are bad overall, even companies that are doing well become apprehensive about the future. I know somewhere in the hierarchy of a large petroleum company, there's a pencil pusher who's saying, "This level of profits can't last forever. We've got to make cutbacks now to prepare."

Frankly, while I just said "pencil pusher" in a derisive manner, it's really hard to find fault with that type of reaction. It's almost impossible not to fall into a funk during a recession if you read a newspaper everyday. The companies may change, but the headlines remain the same. In a downturn, people get laid off. If it's not the Big Three domestic auto companies, it's a computer manufacturer or a bank or "Whatever!"

And if it's not layoffs, it's cutbacks, raising prices, fewer services. It's hard not to believe that economic disaster is just around the corner, and it's extremely difficult and counterintuitive for corporate executives not to react.

It's hard for executives even at companies that are doing well to get excited about spending a lot of money. Even if they don't anticipate hard times ahead, their instinct is to be cautious about expenses. And the more far-sighted among them wait for something bad to happen, though there's no reason in the world that that will happen—except of course their belief in the negative media reports.

> *It's hard for executives even at companies*
> *that are doing well to get excited*
> *about spending a lot of money.*

So here's my next big tip: Negativity feeds on negativity. You don't have to remember that or write it down—because I will be repeating it on a regular basis for the remainder of the book.

CASE IN POINT

I know one very large company that created a committee to review every purchase over $100,000—a sum that director-level executives used to be able to approve on their own. In the past, the executive merely had to approve the spending; since it was at his level there was no need to go further. Now all of that has changed. There are more review committees and the purchasing agent has become even more powerful than before. I guess to some degree that isn't so bad for the company. For those of who sell, this makes our job that much more difficult. A sales guy told me that he found himself "selling" to the Chief Information Officer a product that the man knew nothing about. He wasn't the end user, the one who usually make the purchase. He sat there for forty-five minutes trying to understand how the end users really work. The conclusion was that the sale went through, but only after the CIO had meeting after meeting with the end users to figure out their job! That says that everyone is under scrutiny. ✦

People like Frank, who once were willing—even eager—to provide money for pilot programs now think twice about renewing existing programs that have been deemed successful for years and years.

All this doesn't mean selling is impossible. It just means it's more difficult. But there's a lot you can do to improve your chances of clinching the deal. Just read on.

Take Action

1. Read about what's happening locally, nationally, and (given the global economy) all around the world and think about how it affects your sales landscape.

2. Check your clients' stock prices (if they're publicly held companies) and evaluate their trends over several weeks before you call on them.

3. Keep a news file of information on each of your clients, including material from business publications (*BusinessWeek*, the *Wall Street Journal, Investor's Business Daily*), newspapers and magazines, and the Internet.

Chapter 2

Break Into the New Selling Environment

Once you know why companies are slowing down in their buying, you can start to plan a strategy for continuing to sell to them. The results can be dramatic.

Two days before I started working on this chapter I got a call from Bill—and the biggest training contract I've landed in more than a decade.

While the economic world around me was crumbling, I landed a deal that essentially makes my year. And next year, too. And if I do a good job, perhaps the year after that as well.

I'm not telling you this to gloat—well, not only to gloat—but to illustrate an important point that is a version of a famous quote by Tip O'Neill. O'Neill, for those of you too young to remember, was one of the last great Boston Irish politicians. He ended up Speaker of the House of Representatives during the Reagan era, and was a significant mover and shaker who understood deal making—and how to get re-elected. What he said was: "All politics is local."

What he meant was that voters really don't care what their Congresspeople do about world problems—the Mideast crisis, poverty in sub-Saharan Africa, and so on. But the people are very aware of jobs the representative brings to his district, of the money for special projects he gets for his community and of the local bar mitzvahs and confirmations he or she attends.

With apologies to O'Neill, I maintain that all sales are local. By that, of course, I mean while the world economy is in a slide toward the doldrums, there are still companies doing well. And even companies that are not doing as well as they once did need supplies, consultants, and equipment. In the midst of chaos, you could be doing well.

> *All sales are local.*

The important thing is to put national and international news about tough times in some kind of perspective. The economy as a whole may be in a downturn, but individual businesses and industries may be seeing an uptick in sales. That's where you'll find opportunities.

Sales Tactic

It can be tough to keep up your enthusiasm when everyone around you is feeling like a kicked puppy. But it's essential. Before you go into any room, before you start any meeting, take a deep breath and expel it. That's right. Fill your lungs with clean air—as clean as it gets around the office—and push it out. As you do so, set aside all the reservations, preconceptions, and other mental baggage that weigh people down. Whatever the circumstances, try to start with a positive statement. You'll find that makes things a lot easier.

As a general rule, a lot of what you achieve is a function of your attitude. If you have the best product in your category, unparalleled service, and the lowest cost, you'll still lose sales you should have made if you come into a meeting with a negative attitude. No one likes to be around negative vibes, and it will turn off customers and prospects; it will blind them to your products' good points.

By the same token, the opposite is true as well. If you walk into a meeting with a positive attitude, it spreads. Enthusiasm is contagious. I know this sounds a bit like psychobabble, something out of the Dr. Phil Book of Sales. But it's true.

It's true when the economy is good. But it is especially true when the economy is on the skids. For one thing, a general air of gloom pervades everywhere. Pretty much everyone is sending out negative vibes—including your customers. So if you can somehow channel positive energy, you'll stand out. You'll be welcome in the office.

One of the toughest industries right now is the newspaper business. Papers are failing at an alarming rate, and layoffs are massive. But one editor who retired sent this note to his former staffers:

"Don't check your courage when you walk in this building. Yes, these are scary times, but it's YOUR decision whether to act frightened. You can get so consumed with what might happen, it can paralyze you. Believe me, I know."

The moment I read it I thought of our situation. It's easy to be caught up in negative hoopla. It's easy to fall into what I call paralysis by analysis. It's easy to blame everything bad that happens on the economy. It's easy, but largely inaccurate. Because even in the worst of times you are far more in control of your destiny than you imagined.

CASE IN POINT

Let me give you an example. Diving is one of my favorite events in the summer Olympics. I watched the competition from Beijing and marveled at how brave these young men and women are. I know my view was only two-dimensional, but from where I sat by a high-definition TV, it looked as though they jumped up and passed only inches from the diving board.

All of them paused for a few seconds before they jumped. I don't want to ascribe a motive for any brief hesitation. Maybe that's the way they're all taught at diving school: stop, get into the moment, jump. Maybe it's a way they get over the butterflies in their stomachs. Whatever.

But one competitor seemed to freeze up there. He stood still for what seemed like an inordinate amount of time. I'm not sure what went through his mind. But suppose he remained frozen and didn't jump? I'm sure that must happen, especially to younger divers. But he did jump after the brief delay and did well—though he didn't win a medal. Still, he was in the game. ✦

Selling is a form of competition, and if you spend all your time worrying about the horrible state of the economy, you won't be on the same level as other salespeople. That's paralysis by analysis. It's a tired and obnoxious expression—but it is true. Sadly.

You have to behave as if you were in the midst of a bull market. You're not. But you have to temper your negative feelings with the understanding that there are people out there buying your product or service and you just have to find them. Also, what goes around comes around. The economy is cyclical, and what goes down must come up. More about attitude in the next chapter.

Take Action

1. Before making a sales call, list five positive things you can say to the client about his business. Write the items on the list as quickly as possible, without stopping to analyze them. List more if you can.

2. Now do the same thing about your product or service. Again, do this quickly and don't overthink it.

3. Remember above all when making a sales call—whether it's to a new or old client, a scheduled visit or a cold call—all sales are local. The opportunities are out there, if you know how to look for them.

Chapter 3

Improve Your Attitude—Or I Wish I Were Dr. Phil

I recently completed a coaching assignment for a large division of a super-large international corporation. I can't give you any details that might help you identify the company, but I will tell you that the division I worked with was badly affected by the unprecedented rise in the price of petroleum.

This company had a small but very professional sales force. However, it was experiencing difficulties overcoming client objections to the price increases it had instituted because of the substantially higher cost of raw materials.

My job was to try to figure out why the company's experienced and talented sales force couldn't successfully overcome clients' disapproval as they'd done many times in the past. To do so, I spent several days with each of the company's top five sales reps. They'd been with the firm an average of nineteen years. The "newest" of the reps had fifteen years of experience selling this particular product.

Each had been among the company's top producers for more than a decade. They only changed the order in which they led the company in sales. But all were down substantially from the year before—more than the company average. It was mystifying and frankly took me an unusually long time to figure out.

What I discovered was that they'd been doing what they'd been doing with the same people for too long and the relationships they'd built with their clients had become too close.

Whoa. What's that you say, Steve? Having a good relationship with your client is *not* a good thing? No . . . and yes. Having a good relationship with a client is not good, it's great. Usually. But there are times when you have to step back and re-examine your priorities.

What each of the sales reps was doing was being too empathetic about the buyers' perceived problems and weren't sufficiently focusing on their own difficulties.

> *There are times when you have to*
> *step back and re-examine your priorities.*

The problem was that many of the clients these reps called on were also hurt by the inflationary effect of increased oil prices; some were in extremely bad—almost precarious—positions.

So the sales reps I worked with became too understanding of their clients' problems.

- Yes, of course I understand why you're switching to an overseas supplier. It's a rough world out there and you have to save every penny you can.
- Of course, I understand that you have to see other suppliers.
- I understand. I understand. I understand.

Baloney! Your job isn't to understand why you are losing business from long-established clients. *Your job is to keep that business for your firm, to expand that business, no matter the economic climate.*

Of course, it's difficult for you not to be sympathetic about the problems of someone you've been doing business with a long time. But the truth is that it will be harder on your family if you lose your objectivity and aggressiveness about the account. Your good relationship may actually drag you down the tubes.

I suggested the company switch the sales reps' accounts around on the theory that these highly skilled and motivated reps are likely to push just a little harder with people they are less emotionally vested in. It's too early to say if this is going to work, though early indications are positive. In the first months after accounts were switched, sales were up 18 percent.

The important lesson here isn't that we should all be exchanging accounts with coworkers. The important lesson is that all of us have to be aware of how easy it is to become less aggressive during bad times—exactly when we should be becoming more ferocious. That you are conscious of the possibility is a step in the right direction toward an attitude readjustment.

CASE IN POINT

Another client sells glass film for blast protection to the U.S. government. The salespeople have been selling to the same agencies (though not necessarily the same contact) for twenty years now. Business was relatively steady, zoomed following the tragedy of 9/11, and recently contracted because of burgeoning federal deficits.

I followed several of this company's salespeople around, too, and what I noticed immediately is that the sales reps were making perfunctory calls, assuming that there was no money available and that there would not be a sale. It seemed their primary interest was to be able to write a call report proving that they were there—and, hence, doing their jobs.

But if they'd looked a little further, examined the government's budget, read a newspaper, they'd have noted that there seems to be plenty of money available to reconstruct Iraq. And, frankly, what area of the world is a more likely candidate for bomb-protected glass?

But rather than venture into new territory, these sales reps were happy to wallow in defeat. After all, they had a handy excuse for not selling: the economy is bad and there is a massive federal deficit. They go in anticipating "no," and that becomes a self-fulfilling prophecy. Negativity doesn't sell. ✦

Dr. Phil Moments

Honest to goodness, I had a sales rep come in and say to me, I know the economy is bad and you probably don't want to buy now, but I thought I'd give a shot. He came off as a sad sack, and even if I needed the product he was selling I wouldn't buy it from him.

I can't emphasize enough how your negativity will hurt your business.

Part of the problem, I think, is that sales reps are used to agreeing with their customers, figuring the less waves they make, the greater the likelihood of a sale. But if the buyer interrupts your pitch by complaining how bad the economy is, your job isn't to agree or be sympathetic to his or her plight. Your job is to figure out a way to overcome that objection.

> *Negativity will hurt your business.*

Look, no one knows your product better than you do. Moreover, you are like a bee, going from company to company, finding out what others are doing. The chances are you're more up-to-date on what's going on in the industry than an average line person. You have the know-how to pollinate that company with ideas you've seen elsewhere.

A good salesperson comes to a client not only with product but also with ideas on how to use them. If your idea well has dried up because you believe that the economy is so bad that you're not going to make a sale anyway, well then, of course, you're not going to make the sale.

So how do you stay positive when all around you are abandoning ship? I've read a lot of self-help books that provide saccharine advice such as:

- Get up every day with a smile on your face.
- Never give up, no matter what.
- Stop whining!

I must confess that there were times I used variations of these same words to motivate my students. But it didn't work. It just was too ephemeral, and what these students—and I presume you—need is something concrete.

However, there are two pieces of wispy Dr. Phil–type suggestions I'd like to make:

Sales Tactic

1. You have to believe in yourself, your product, and the idea that you are bringing the best possible deal to your customer. You've got to believe that you're genuinely making a difference. If you really don't think you can make a difference in your customers' lives, then perhaps you're in the wrong business—or at least working for the wrong company. If you don't feel positive about what you do, then you're just going through the motions. It's just a job, and no one likes to work. I say this to all my students no matter the economy. But the words sound a little more forced in bad times. There aren't many jobs around; people aren't hiring.

I understand that. But there's no reason you can't find something positive about your situation, and focus on that.

2. You've been given lemons. Make lemonade. Talk about stock advice. But it's true. Sure, a bad economy is a burden, but it's also an opportunity. Nothing is working, so why not try something new? See if you can expand your traditional marketing focus beyond existing industries. See if you can come up with innovative pricing and delivery policies and get your bosses to improve them. Kris Kristofferson wrote one of my favorite songs, "Me and Bobby McGee." In it he says, "Freedom's just another word for nothing left to lose." And he's right. With the economy so bad, you have nothing left to lose. You're free to soar. ✦

Take Action

1. Make a list of five new places you've never sold to before and cold call them for appointments.

2. If sales are lagging, talk to one of your coworkers about switching clients for a while, to give and get a fresh perspective. If you don't want to actually switch accounts, do some role playing, with your coworker playing his client.

3. Make a list of the top five excuses you hear from accounts and write down your strongest counterarguments. Be sure to use those arguments the next time you talk to your accounts.

Chapter 4

You Need a Personal Business Plan

One of the things I always tell students is that they need a business plan in the same way that a company does. It just needs to be built around the "You Corporation"—or, perhaps more accurately, the "Me Corporation."

In either case, whether you are a company or an individual, you need to have a vision of the future. Life is a road trip. You can't expect to reach your destination in a timely manner—or at all for that matter—if you drive around aimlessly. You have to decide where you want to go, put the address in your GPS, and get going.

Simply put, everyone should have a business plan. Sure, it's possible to go through life without one and still be successful. I'm sure there are many people who have done that, wandering from job to job taking life as it comes. And I'm also sure if you keep buying lottery tickets, you'll win the big prize. In fact, the money is only one drawing away, so figure this time next week you'll be in clover. (It's difficult when I'm writing to be certain you understand my tone. I'm being sarcastic, people.)

But, new found fortune aside, the truth is that I'd put my money on a person who has a vision of what he or she wants to accomplish in life and stays focused on it.

This is more important in bad times than when things are going well. When times are good, when the economy is pushing full speed ahead on all cylinders, everybody makes sales. Everybody. But it's times when venerable financial institutions are failing left and right, the stock market is hitting record lows, housing prices are falling like a rock, and no one knows who is next that you especially need a plan.

> *Everyone should have*
> *a business plan.*

Also, I remember reading a bunch of years ago about a study conducted by an Ivy League university. It concluded that people who write things down—those who make notes for themselves, who have to-do lists—are far more likely to be successful than people who don't. I can't cite chapter and verse of this, so you'll have to take my word for it, but it makes sense to me. These folks are better organized and better prepared to meet the exigencies of what the day holds for them. And a business plan is essentially nothing more than a long-term to-do list.

What is a business plan? It is an encapsulation of your life—both business and personal. It describes where you are now, where you want to go, and how you intend to get there.

What does a business plan have to do with your personal life? The answer is uncomplicated: For any plan to work it needs to be realistic. Some people feel their jobs are more important than anything else. They want—they need—to succeed. Much of their self-esteem is tied to their successes at work. They are prepared to make whatever sacrifices are necessary to reach the top—and if that means working eighty hours a week, so be it.

On the other hand, there are good salespeople who have different priorities, and don't care if they are the highest-paid reps in the office—not if it means putting in all that time. So if the goals set down in your plan are going to be realistic (and in large measure by realistic I mean attainable) they have to take into account factors outside the industry—including your willingness to put in a lot of hours.

(And don't for one minute think I'm critical of people for whom work is not the be-all and end-all. In some ways, I admire them. I don't for one second believe that there are a lot of people in any profession who get to the Pearly Gates and tell St. Peter, "If only I'd spent more time at work.")

Putting down pie-in-the-sky goals you can't possibly meet can only serve to discourage you. On the other hand, consistently meeting realistic goals not only is encouraging, but also is an indication that you can do so much more.

One of the great things about business plans is that they serve as excellent benchmarks of where you've been. What did I hope to accomplish when I first wrote a plan two years ago? Did I do it? Did I get close? Did the modifications I've added since then work for me, or am I just spinning my wheels? Has anything changed in my personal life that requires me to readjust my professional goals?

Well, you might ask, what's the point of having a plan if you have to keep changing it? Or, put metaphorically, is a plan a plan if the only plan is to change the plan? Good question that I'll answer with another: What's the point of sticking to a plan when the environment in which it was created has changed? Frankly, I believe a business plan is only good the first day of a start-up. I exaggerate, but just a little. In today's global economy, things change so quickly that the Me Company can get mired in a plan that is antiquated without knowing it. Your business plan has to be re-examined on a regular basis and adjusted as needed.

Which brings us to the thrust of this book—how to sell in bad times. More than anything else, a business plan forces you to focus. As I said just a few paragraphs ago, you can see how you're doing.

Sales Tactic

When times are bad and sales are down, it's time to con-

duct a review of the way you operate. We all know it's easy

to adopt a times-are-bad-there's-nothing-I-can-do-about-it

attitude. But that doesn't get you anywhere. You need a business plan to give you direction.

Set aside some time when you won't be interrupted. You'll need to be very detailed and very honest with yourself. Go somewhere where there are no distractions: ringing phones, chirping computers, and so forth.

When you're done with the plan, set it aside for a day; then come back to it and make changes.

So, what is your business plan going to look like?

The first thing you need to do is examine past incarnations of your plan. (If you don't have a plan and have read this far, you understand that now would be a good time to start one.) Look at what you wrote and see what's worked for you in the past. Was there a time when you noted that you had to concentrate on former clients, worked at it, and then as sales picked up sort of let that part of your operation lie fallow? Maybe now would be a good time to pick up on that again.

Another possibility: Have you mined your inner Willie Sutton? Sutton once said that he robbed banks because that's where the money was. As I noted previously, all sales are local. Sure the economy is down the tubes. But not everyone is affected in the same way. There are pockets of profits out there, and if you put your mind to it there probably is a way you can share in them

Let me give you an example. The American automobile industry is not doing well now. But many foreign manufacturers are, so if you make engine parts, you (or someone at your company) are already probably in contact with representatives of Toyota or Honda. That's obvious. But a bad economy means people have less disposable income. Many may not renew their contracts with lawn services next summer, opting to cut their own grass.

Could that mean lawn mower sales will increase? Do you have a part that might fit or be adapted to a lawn mower engine? Obviously

I just made this up to illustrate a point I made in the last chapter. Or actually Kris Kristofferson made: Freedom's just another word for nothin' left to lose.

Sales are down; you're free to soar, to go places and try ideas your bosses would never allow when business was good. When General Motors and Ford were keeping your factories humming, why waste time on Briggs & Stratton?

But now you have nothing but time. Use it creatively.

Make Lemonade

Here's an example from a non-sales environment to show you what I mean. A writer friend of mine was dramatically affected by the down-turn in the markets at the turn of the century. His biggest client was a large financial newspaper with which he had a contract to write three articles every two weeks. It was his meat and potatoes, the contract that provided him with his essentials and some time to do some additional writing elsewhere for the extras. He'd been with them for a while when the markets plunged. Advertising in this newspaper plummeted.

Use your time

creatively.

The "contract" was unilaterally changed. Instead of relying on freelancers as much as they had in the past, editors would now be required to assign more to staff writers. My friend went from three articles every two weeks to one article every three weeks—effectively losing about three-quarters of his income.

Clearly my friend was devastated. But he decided he'd make lemonade. He occasionally taught a class at a local high school adult education extension on nonfiction article writing. He'd adapted his night school class curriculum from article writing to business writing, and had delivered it successfully a couple of times. But he had never really marketed the course; he considered himself a writer, not a writing teacher—until his freelance writing universe collapsed.

He told me: "I figured I had nothing left to lose. If I wasn't going to promote the course then, when I had time, I'd never do it." He joined a couple of training organizations and picked up some helpful marketing hints. He networked with almost everyone he knew. And eventually, through a friend, he managed to land a presentation at a large consulting/accounting firm.

He was overjoyed, until he realized he'd never delivered a presentation before. He was usually at the other end; people presented their stories to him. But he marched bravely ahead—and failed miserably.

It was a wake-up call. He focused on creating a good presentation. He honed it down to less than a half hour and began to have some successes. He changed his course dramatically, offering both one- and two-day modules to fit the needs of different clients. He did brand extensions—offering a basic grammar course and then adding a refresher course for people who'd taken the basic writing course.

And it worked. He couldn't retire on what he earned as a writing teacher, but it became a valuable supplement to his freelancing. There were a couple of years where teaching provided a substantial percentage of his income.

You can do the same thing. And in the following chapters I'm going to show you how.

Take Action

1. Write a five-point business plan, setting out goals and attaching a timetable to each one.

2. In six months, evaluate your business plan. How many goals have you achieved? How many are you part way to achieving? Are you keeping to your schedule? What other goals should you set for yourself to replace the ones you've accomplished.

3. Pick a negative thing about your sales landscape and brainstorm three or four ways to turn it into a positive thing.

Chapter 5

Can You Change?

I'm going to throw a little science at you. I assume most of you are familiar with Darwin's theory of evolution. You know: survival of the fittest. Because it has a direct application to sales—especially in an unhealthy sales environment—I've renamed it Darwin's Theory of Sales-Solutions.

It's important to note that Darwin never said "survival of the biggest" or the "strongest" or the "swiftest." He said survival was based on being the fittest. And the classic example of what Darwin meant is the story of a species of moth in Industrial-Age England.

The moth was very common in its "peppered" coloration—mostly white with black spots—while its all-black cousin was a rarity. But the nation was in the midst of a revolutionary change at the time, from individual artisans to a factory-based economy. And these new factories were spewing coal dust all over the previously pristine countryside. While this had its advantages for working-class people, who suddenly had a lot of opportunity, it wreaked havoc on the white moths. Trees that previously had provided a level of camouflage for the white moths were now black with soot, making the moths easy targets for predators.

Now it was the black moths that had the benefit of camouflage, and they survived in much greater numbers, passing their genes on to future generations. And over a matter of time, as predators ate more and more white moths and left the black ones alone, the black moths became dominant. Therein lies Darwin's definition of survival of the fittest: the fittest are those best able to thrive in the changing environment. The business environment is changing. The question is, can you adapt or do you become extinct?

In previous chapters I've spoken about changes in the way in which you sell. That is, you have to approach your clients and potential clients in a more uninhibited manner. You have to ignore limits that you or your company's management previously placed on you. To mix my metaphors, you have to become a Trekkie and go where no sales reps have gone before.

This Herculean change in methodology requires a significant attitudinal change—and frankly not everyone is capable of adapting. Some will just give up. No matter how hard their managers try to help them, they'll prove incapable of selling in the new environment. I've been a white moth all my life, they say. I'm too old to change. For them the glass isn't half empty or half full; it's bone dry.

Others will consider the glass half empty and will at least try to make the change. But they won't be able to.

But if you are a glass-half-full kind of person, then you come preprogrammed to make this type of attitudinal change. Even better (and I've met only a few people like this in my entire life), not only do you see the glass as half full, but you also offer to run to the fountain to fill it to the brim.

There are several key ingredients to survival in bad times. I've already discussed some of them: imagination and creativity, the ability to think outside the box, understanding time management. But I don't think any is as important as your willingness to change, to maintain a positive attitude in the face of everything declining.

Sales Tactic

Sometimes it's good to do a SWOT analysis. SWOT is a business acronym, standing for Strengths, Weaknesses, Opportunities, Threats.

On a sheet of paper, list your strengths. Give yourself a big pat on the back; you deserve it. Then list your weaknesses—and be honest.

Now comes the challenging part. Make a list of the opportunities you see in your sales landscape. You might need to take a while on this. Maybe put it aside for a day and then come back to it. When you've finished—or at least got a healthy list—make another list of possible threats. These could range from the economy getting worse to your products falling behind the curve.

Seen altogether, these four elements can help you look positively at your situation and not fall into the glass-half-empty trap.

Even if things are well for you personally and your company, it's hard not to succumb to the economy blues. How do you not succumb to melancholy when every day the paper reports another round of layoffs, companies filing for bankruptcy, or shutting down altogether. It becomes a self-fulfilling prophecy.

The business environment is changing.
The question is, can you adapt?

The black moths survived by being different, and so can you—by being positive, ignoring the conventional wisdom that says all is lost.

If you can do that, you'll be able to maintain the two requisite components to success as a rep: persistence and consistency. When I give my classes and speeches, these are the things I usually stress.

Keep Up Persistence and Consistency

Persistence means that you keep going straight ahead on the sales highway when it seems as though it makes more sense to veer off for a rest stop. No one said it was going to be easy. But you improve your odds of success just by being there while many of your competitors give up.

> *Persistence means going straight*
> *ahead on the sales highway.*

Consistency is equally important. I recently went to see an ear, nose, and throat doctor, a friend of mine, because I felt an occasional pain in my left ear. When he examined me, however, he looked in my right ear. I knew him well enough to ask, "What part of pain in my left ear did you not understand?"

His response: "I always start on the right side no matter the complaint. It's a pattern I developed so I don't miss anything."

Coincidentally, I had an appointment the following day with my dental hygienist. I asked her about it and, yes, she too, cleans teeth the same way every time, from left to right, top first, bottom next. It made sense to me. And, in fact, was something I've consistently tried to do myself.

I schedule time every day to prospect. I schedule time every day to work on upcoming presentations. I schedule time every day to schedule my next day, my next week, my next month. For me, there's something comforting in that type of consistency. And while I occasionally slip off the wagon, I always return, because consistency is comforting to me.

You need to focus on persistence and consistency if you're going to get through an economic downturn. Above all, you have to avoid becoming a white moth. Your ability to adapt to a down economy is the key

Take Action

1. Don't listen to naysayers. They seem to be everywhere and are difficult to ignore. I just concentrate on the positive. The economy may stink, but I'm doing fine. So maybe the naysayers are wrong. In short: find something positive to focus on to combat the negativity all around you.

2. Do something that makes you feel good for yourself and about yourself. Buy a new suit. Buy a large-screen TV. Reward yourself in advance for the success you are about to have.

3. Make sure you look good every single day, no matter how you feel. Truth: looking good will make you feel good.

4. Find some alone time during the day, away from the phones, away from colleagues, to just think. No lunch appointment. Don't eat at your desk. Buy yourself a nice lunch. Treat yourself as though you were a client.

5. Leave the office in the office. Don't bring it home to your family.

Chapter 6

Evaluate Your Skills

I think that too often in an age when computers do everything for us from scheduling to creating lavish presentations we lose sight of something important: This is a people business. It isn't a computer talking electronically to another computer to get a contract. It is a person—you—speaking to other people who need to make a connection.

So it's important to understand that a key ingredient in a business plan is you. At the same time that you re-evaluate your goals in terms of the economy, you also have to evaluate the skills you bring to the table.

> *A key ingredient in a*
> *business plan is you.*

You must examine your own strengths and weaknesses and how they affect your ability to meet your business goals. Do you, for example, possess any of the following traits?

Are you *energetic?* Do you keep moving forward in a positive manner, or do you tire quickly? Energy is almost always positive, so this is a key attribute. Dragging yourself into a prospect's office is not a way to instill confidence in you or what you are selling. A recurring theme in this book is the need to be positive. That includes your energy level and even the way you dress. You come in tie askew, suit not pressed, shoes not shined and you signal to prospects that you are not the kind of person they want to deal with. This seems so basic it hardly bears mentioning, but it is easy to overlook details—and get depressed—when you're focused on reversing a downturn in sales. Don't let that happen to you.

Are you *young at heart* if not age? This is a youth-oriented society. If you act old (no mater your age) people will consider you a relic. By that I don't mean you have to come in with your hair in a ponytail (man or woman) spouting hip-hop lyrics. But you don't want to spend the bulk of your time talking about the good old days and the time you played golf with Ike. No one cares, and, in fact, I'd bet a lot of younger people have no idea who Ike is. (It's President Eisenhower, if you're interested.) At the very least, you should be aware of what's going on in popular culture today—films, television, books, and theater—because that is an easy way to get a conversation going.

Are you *self-motivated*? Can you work independently, or do you need a manager standing over your shoulder pushing you?

Do you have *forceful persuasion techniques*? Can you construct well-thought-out, intelligent, and convincing arguments for why a company should use your product or service? If you consistently get to make presentations but rarely get over the hump to actually closing a sale, something is likely wrong in the way you present. There are several good books on sales presentation techniques, including *Sales Presentation Techniques That Really Work!* Modesty forbids me from mentioning the author of that book.

Do you possess good *communication skills*? That is, do you speak and write well? You may be the best sales rep in the world, but if you can't communicate your thoughts, you're no better than the worst sales rep. Your speech and writing must be grammatically correct. It needs to be well organized.

Do you *understand your business*? By that I mean more than the basics; I mean the subtleties: how and why people make decisions, how the global economy impacts you, how internal politics may determine who gets the contract.

Do you have a sense of *entrepreneurship*? Do you feel like you own your piece of business? If you do, act accordingly to protect your interests. If you don't, buy in. Your commission checks are a piece of the action, and you need to act like an owner to protect them.

Are you *honest*? And by honest, I also mean realistic. Can you truthfully evaluate your skills? If you can do so sincerely and candidly, you're in great shape. Because . . .

Are you *able to learn*? That is are you the type of person who recognizes his or her own strengths and weaknesses? If so, then you are probably the person who will work to improve areas where you are imperfect.

Once you've analyzed these aspects of yourself (and you can do a lot of this in the SWOT analysis mentioned in the previous chapter), you'll be better positioned to take advantage of the opportunities a downturn offers. That's right—I said, opportunities.

Nothing to Lose

In the last couple of chapters I've spoken to you about what I feel is a potentially positive outgrowth of an economic downturn. That is, if sales are going down the tubes, it really frees you up to be innovative, to try something different, if only because you have nothing to lose.

In the case of my writer friend, he put some effort behind an idea he had harbored for a long time but was always too busy to pursue. With several clients cutting back or altogether eliminating freelance writers, he had nothing but time now. He believed in his idea and had nothing to lose.

The example I gave of the engine parts manufacturer was entirely fictional. But it did illustrate the point I was trying to make: When times are good, when sales are high, we tend to keep our thinking entirely within the proverbial box. Sales and commissions are rolling in. Why do anything to upset the apple cart?

But with nothing to lose, you can try something different, something innovative, something that will make you stand out—even if it fails.

CASE IN POINT

Let's imagine that you are the sales rep for the engine parts manufacturer. GM and Ford are your accounts, and as we all know, times have not been good for domestic manufacturers. So you suggest calling on Briggs & Stratton, the small-engine manufacturer. You cold call, you get an appointment, you make progress, but at the last minute, the deal falls through. The company decides to stay with its current supplier.

So what? I repeat, this time in boldface italics, *So what?* You have lost nothing—because you had nothing to lose! It wasn't like you were busy selling another account. No one was buying. Plus, there was a lot of upside.

First of all, if I were your boss I would be extremely impressed by your initiative. While your colleagues were probably crying in their beers, you were out in the marketplace trying to improve the company's business in a creative and entirely new way. That kind of thinking marks you as a comer.

But there are a couple of other potential benefits. Let's suppose you look for a job somewhere down the road. It's something you can point to, an example of the kind of unconventional thinking that future employers are likely to find very attractive.

Finally, don't forget the possibility that the small-engine market will eventually open to you. Just because you got a "no" now doesn't mean that you will tomorrow or next week. I believe that given a choice most companies prefer to deal with consultants rather than sales reps (more on that later). By opening up a new possibility at Briggs & Stratton, you in many ways fill the consultant's role. And when times get better, when small-engine sales pick up, when additional suppliers are being considered, your name and your product will no doubt be thrown into the mix. ✦

Real-World Examples

In essence, swimming against the current, thinking outside the proverbial box in a bad economy turns out to be a win-win-win situation—ironic, since it all started because you had nothing to lose.

In what is considered by many (as this is written) to be the worst economic crisis since the Great Depression, I landed a bunch of new clients by following what I just suggested to you. I landed a large direct-mail company—one of those firms that send out coupons—by suggesting ways they can package exclusive mailings for a single manufacturer. That is, do a mailing devoted to coupons of, say, Proctor & Gamble products or Kraft Foods.

Based on my discussions with the company president and several of his clients, I thought at least two or three coupon-oriented conglomerates would be willing to pay a little extra to ensure that no competitors' products were in the same mailing. One of the company's clients I visited, in fact, was so excited by the idea that he offered to contact other product managers to get them involved. He said he was sure the company wouldn't sign a long-term contract, but almost certainly would experiment with the idea. And if it worked, he was certain there'd be much more business in it for my client.

Sounds wonderful, right? What more could you want while the economy around you is in shambles? The problem—and this amazes me—is that the sales manager didn't buy into the idea. First, he thought it wouldn't work. Second, he said a lot of different reps had pieces of the client's business and it was too much trouble to reorganize everything. Third, he thought that even if it was successful, it might alienate many current customers.

That reaction defied logic. The company's business was flat to down and heading further south. Sure, reorganizing might be a pain in the, uh, neck. Yes, the neck. But here you had a potentially sizable amount of new business that should have made it worthwhile.

Moreover, that some existing customers might be upset is a specious argument. Why would they be upset? In fact, they might be happy that their all-purpose cleanser no longer had to compete with Brand X all-purpose cleanser, because Brand X was now in a separate mailing.

My guess is that the sales manager just didn't want to put in the extra hours. And he probably wasn't hot about the idea of implementing someone else's concept—for which someone else would get credit. Unfortunately, the company's president bought into the sales manager's argument. Did I mention that they were related? Did I mention that blood is thicker than added sales?

My point here is don't you be the naysayer. The sales manager should have endorsed the idea because he really had nothing to lose! Except now, if someone else buys into the concept and it works, he'll lose credibility (at the least) and maybe his job. Blood is thicker than added sales, but not so much against added profits.

> *Don't be*
> *the naysayer!*

So the lesson to be learned here is you should be creative, you should be imaginative, and you should be open to new ideas—even if they're not yours.

Here is an example of what I mean about positive attitude. A company that distributes water coolers found that people weren't buying new water coolers in a stagnant economy. This was not one of those coolers where you had to replace the bottles every day, so there was no continuing revenue source other than occasional service calls or the purchase of replacement coolers. However, the company did make a little bit of money on the special cups it supplied, cups that were biodegradable and suitable for either hot or cold water. It provided them almost at cost as a service.

In investigating the company and its clients, I found that many of its coolers were installed in the offices of large companies, companies that I would want to reach with my message if I could. And then I had a brainstorm. Why not sell tiny ads on the cups. Again, it seemed to me like a win-win-win situation.

Advertisers could deliver a message to companies where they may not have had easy access before. I found an advertising sales rep company that worked exclusively on commission. The folks there loved the idea. Thought it was a great new revenue stream for them. My client loved the idea because there was no out-of-pocket expense. The company had nothing to lose! And everything to gain.

Innovation Gets It Done

Not only did the company, too, now have a potentially decent new revenue stream, but it also had a great marketing tool. When its reps sold new coolers, one of the chief selling points was that the customer didn't have additional costs for replacing the water. Now the company could say its customers didn't even have to pay for cups.

I make this sound a lot simpler than it really was. From the moment I broached the idea to my client until the first advertising cups were actually in use was a period of about nine months. My client had to be convinced that this would work and that there were tangible benefits in it for his company. The same held true for the sales rep company I found. Yes, they liked the idea, but they had to be convinced it would work before top executives would commit to it. Finally, the advertisers were reluctant to participate.

Advertising agencies always are resistant to trying anything new and untested. So the sales reps had to do end-arounds to get companies to pay for this out of a marketing budget rather than the ad budget. But eventually a couple of hardy corporate souls signed on, and that was close enough for break-even so that everyone involved breathed a deep sigh of relief.

As I sit down to right this, all the signs look good. We're close to signing a couple of additional advertisers and everyone appears pleased, especially me.

I got this consulting contract because I was able to approach the company with an idea that differentiated me from the pack. It allowed me to soar.

Take Action

1. Make a list of your skills and examine your strengths and weaknesses. Be honest with yourself—the more straightforward you are, the better use you'll make of the tools at your disposal.

2. When confronted by any new problem or obstacle, start by thinking of the wackiest, most out-of-the-box solution possible. Then ask yourself why that solution wouldn't work. If you can't think of a reason, give it a try.

3. Look for ideas that are creative and different from what everyone else is proposing. Remember that sometimes the best ideas come from combining two completely different concepts.

Chapter 7

Return to the Fount

For most of us, the worst thing about hard economic times is the uncertainty. Everything we've traditionally counted on—from a steady paycheck to a comfortable life—is up in the air when the, uh, economy hits the fan.

In hard or harder times it is especially important that sales reps take stock of their books. When it comes to existing accounts, the conventional wisdom is that unless you somehow screw things up:

1. A good account will likely be yours for your entire career.

2. They are the best place to go when you want/need additional business.

Under normal circumstances, I would agree with the conventional wisdom. Most people operate on the theory that "the devil you know is better than the devil you don't know." That is, you get used to working with a sales rep and a supplier, you get into a comfort zone, and it is easier to stay in that comfort zone than start all over with new people and new companies.

Of course, it never guaranteed that suppliers would retain their accounts, but it certainly improved the odds.

The same held true with getting additional business. You, the sales rep, already have the contacts and the (presumably good) relationship with the company. If an opportunity comes up, why wouldn't your contacts steer the business to you? Since you are probably on the client's site a lot, why wouldn't you hear about possible openings for your product or service well before a competitor?

> *When people are concerned*
> *about their own future . . .*
> *loyalty is out the window.*

But when the economy is off, all bets are off, too. When people are concerned about their own future, about the company's, about paying for gasoline or the mortgage, loyalty is out the window. Remember, your contact and his or her company are more concerned with self-preservation than yours.

So where does that leave you? Hopefully it leaves you soaring. Again. By soaring, I mean breaking out of your cage and finding new ways to sell. Flying so high that you can see the whole sales landscape spread out below you, and you can see clearly where the opportunities are.

Sales Tactic

A great way to soar is to get your client to discard his or her image of you as a sales rep, supplier, or vendor. Instead, you want to substitute the impression that you are a trusted advisor and consultant.

I was brought in by a large metropolitan daily. Sales were flat to down (common among American newspapers) and the idea was that I would imbue the paper's sales force with new concepts. I'd worked with the paper's publisher when she was in a different job years ago, so, not surprisingly, when sales started to level off and then turn south she thought of me.

What I typically do in cases like this is spend some time examining the market, going out on calls with sales reps and generally getting a better idea of what's going on. Even though we'd worked together before, I think she was very surprised by what I reported. I told her:

"Your sales force seems pretty good. I can give them a class or two, but I don't think that's the problem."

I spent the next hour or so talking myself out of a lucrative training contract. I told her the economy is hurting her more than anything else, and there was little I could do to change that. She already knew that newspapers were cutting back left and right; I just told her that training an already-competent sales force wasn't the way to go.

Instead, I suggested the paper concentrate additional resources on developing new product lines. One idea I had was to emphasize special sections. Not that these special sections are a new idea. But traditionally this paper waited for a client to propose one. I suggested that the paper go out and market the idea. For example, some of the daily's traditional (and major) sources of revenue were city agencies; they advertised for everything from bid opportunities to how great a job they were doing.

But because of the bad economy, the mayor had ordered every city agency to slash its budget, and those cutbacks had seriously impacted the paper. Why not try to develop a city special section? It would focus on business opportunities in the city (hoping to attract new industry) and places to see (hoping to attract more tourists). If the city agreed to sponsor the section, it could monitor the editorial content (this was an ad section, not an editorial section) and both the city itself and appropriate agencies would likely advertise.

Better still, with the city's endorsement many private companies would agree to participate as well: real estate agencies with properties to lease, local attractions, restaurants, and theaters.

Another suggestion I had was that in exchange for the city's endorsement and minimal advertising commitment, the paper could promise the mayor 1,000 reprints. I knew that wouldn't be enough for a meaningful promotional effort by the city and so it would have to order more copies—an additional source of revenue for the paper.

This newspaper tried it and it worked out even better than I'd imagined. There were more advertisers than the publisher had budgeted for, and many of them were new advertisers—companies that hadn't advertised in the paper before or hadn't advertised recently.

It's premature to tell whether these sections will generate incremental revenue with potential clients—but it already has for me. The publisher was impressed by my willingness to give up a lucrative training contract rather than run unnecessary classes as well as the acumen I showed in suggesting the advertising supplements. So while I didn't do any training there, she hired me as an advertising sales consultant—which is over the long term at least as lucrative as the original training contract—and has passed my name along to other publishers in her multinewspaper chain.

Will other business result? It's still too early to say. I've just started cold calling between chapters. But the early results are promising. This is a great example of how creative thinking changes you from a vendor to an advisor and imbeds you so far in a company that there's little chance a competitor will get you out. The newspaper is grateful to me for my creative suggestions, and I've transformed their image of me: now I'm not just a sales consultant—I'm the guy who came up with the great ideas that might enable them to save their paper.

CASE IN POINT

Here's another example of what I mean. I do a lot of work with banks, and the commercial business at one of my accounts was relatively flat. It wasn't anything that the company was doing incorrectly. It was just that in a rocky economic landscape, the bank's customers weren't growing, so there was little need for these generally small companies to do more business with the bank.

I'm a sales trainer. But again, training wasn't the proper response. Coincidentally, the bank had recently unsuccessfully pitched a large accounting firm that specialized in helping small businesses. So I suggested a way to kill two birds with one stone. The bank president agreed to refer appropriate small business clients to the accounting firm; in exchange, the accounting firm agreed to offer lower introductory rates for a year.

This was another one of those win-win situations I'm so proud of. Many of the bank's clients were able to increase their business under the accounting firm's guidance. This meant they were able to increase their deposits and business with the bank. And as a final added bonus, the accounting firm's top officers felt so guilty about picking up additional business from my bank that they ultimately moved their accounts there.

In the next chapter, I'll give some additional examples of soaring. ✦

Take Action

1. Consider your top ten accounts. What do you know about their business? What problems do they have? And how could you help them solve those problems? (Don't think exclusively in terms of sales-related issues.)

2. Next time you talk to a customer, ask him his impressions of how his company is weathering the downturn. The more you get him talking, and the more you listen carefully to what he has to say, the closer you are to finding a sales tactic that lets you soar.

3. Check your clients' websites regularly. You need to be aware of problems as soon as possible, and the websites (and any other sources of information you can tap) will give you that edge.

Chapter 8

Soar Higher

In this chapter I intend to provide some additional examples of how soaring can pay off. Why a new chapter? Why not merely make Chapter Eight longer?

Simple. I reread it and sprained my hand patting myself on the back. I figured maybe if I rested a while, I'd be better able to get back to the keyboard without further injury to the hand. I rested and here I am again. This time I'll be careful patting my back.

Seriously, starting a new chapter is an excuse for me to re-emphasize the major points here. This is not just about improving your business, though that's certainly an important part of why you have to think far more creatively with clients. It's certainly not just about making desperation moves in a bad economy, though certainly the desperation a bad economy precipitates frees you up to be creative.

What this really is about is the relationship you have or should have with your clients under all circumstances. When times are good and orders, cash, and commissions flow in like ocean waves at high tide, we tend to take existing clients for granted. This is a reminder that we shouldn't. It's important to imbed ourselves when times are good, because that is something clients remember when times are bad. And they always somehow turn bad.

But more important, this is a reminder that there's always a little more business to be had. Almost all of the solutions I cited in the last chapter and cite here could have been offered in good times, as well.

Anyway, back to patting myself on the back. Actually, not so fast. My favorite story doesn't involve me. A former student sold ball bearings. I'm not entirely sure what they do, but he assures me they're important and omnipresent if not omnipotent.

My friend Joe had a large account that provided a significant share of his business but was not planning on renewing its contract with him and his firm. Instead, it was going to start purchasing ball bearings from a Chinese supplier. Joe's contact was very apologetic, but the client company would enjoy significant savings by moving production overseas.

> *There's always a little more*
> *business to be had.*

Joe had a number of choices, among them Dewars, Jack Daniels, or Beefeater. Surprisingly, he chose another tack. He visited the client company's manufacturing facilities and found that the company inserted the ball bearings into (and I'm going to use the technical term) some kind of circular doodad. He got a sample and brought it back to his own plant. Working with his own manufacturing gurus, the company's marketing department and, eventually, its CEO, the firm came up with a way to take its own ball bearings, insert them into doodads, and deliver the completed part (just in time) to the client company's plant. That innovation saved the account.

This is a perfect example of what I mean by soaring. It turned out to be one of those proverbial win-win situations (except for the Chinese manufacturer). The client company wound up ahead on a number of levels. While it will pay a few pennies more apiece than it would have if it purchased the Chinese-made ball bearing and assembled it themselves, that's more than offset by a number of built-in advantages the new system includes.

First of all, there's a guarantee of quality assurance. As we all know from a batch of headlines, the terms *quality* and *Chinese* are not yet necessarily synonymous. Second, it retains a longtime relationship with a supplier of known quality. And if anything goes wrong or gets damaged, subpar merchandise can be replaced the same day, not two or three weeks—or months—later. Third, there were substantial cost savings associated with just-in-time delivery, which Joe promised. There was no need to lay out funds for products sitting around for weeks waiting to be assembled. Finally, with the extra space now available in its plant (because it doesn't have to warehouse parts and the manufacturing process has been simplified), the company can now increase production without a costly expansion of its plant.

As for Joe's company, they kept a valuable client, who was now spending a little more money with them than before, and created a potentially lucrative new profit center they might be able to offer other clients.

Sweet.

But it's not the end of the story, because these stories don't have ends. Rick Pitino, the future Hall of Fame college basketball coach has a slogan that seems to defy logic: He says if it ain't broke, break it and improve it.

> *"If it ain't broke,*
> *break it and improve it."*

His point is that you can't rest on your laurels. If he comes up with a new wrinkle for his team's offense, some other coach will come up with a new defense to keep Pitino's team, the University of Louisville, from scoring. It's the same with Joe here. Do you for one minute believe that the Chinese manufacturer isn't going to come back with another offer? You have to keep pushing forward. I'm pretty sure the laws of physics keep you from soaring backward.

Some companies have a program called Continuous Quality Improvement. That's fancy talk for something pretty simple: you have to keep innovating, keep improving what you're doing and how you're doing it. Because you can be sure your competitors are doing that.

Soaring is based on the same principle: All those other sales forces out there are trying to find new products to sell to your accounts and better ways of selling them. So if you don't find ways of soaring—*especially* in tough times—you'll be standing on the ground watching your accounts fly off into the distance.

Meanwhile, here are a couple of additional examples that may spark some new flight patterns of your own. The first two involve banks.

CASE IN POINT

For one reason or another, a bank was losing more accounts than it was gaining, and this attrition, if it continued, would threaten its very existence. I was brought in, and I asked the bank's executives what I thought were reasonably logical questions. For example, what do people say when they close their accounts?

I was told they offer a variety of explanations. They were moving. They found a competitor's branch that was much closer. And often, they were upset about something, a surly teller, long lines, low interest rates. But in every case where there was a problem, even if we offered to fix it and added inducements to get them back, the former customers refused.

So it seemed to me that we had to get to these customers before they closed their accounts. I got the bank to do some research, and it seemed there were three traits common to almost all of them. They stopped receiving checks that previously had been deposited electronically (indicating they were going to another bank), they reduced the amount of money in their accounts, and wrote fewer checks.

I suggested that if we could identify these clients early on—
it had to come no later than when the third element was in
place—we might be able to contact them and reverse the
decision.

I created and conducted a quick training program for the
bank's customer service reps and within three months the
bank was able to retain 80 percent of the people identified
as customers likely to leave.

It's no wonder I sprained my hand, is it?

Just in case you thought that was a fluke, here's another example: I cold called a different bank and got an assignment to train
the platform personnel on how to sell more effectively. About two
months after I finished, I met with the bank's president and director
of human resources to see if the training met with their satisfaction.

Their response: yes and no. Sales were up, but a number of
employees were requesting refresher training. They weren't too surprised, because I'd warned them of that possibility. But I suggested,
instead of a one-course-fits-all session, that I visit individual branches
and provide training on that level, dealing with issues particular to
that branch.

As I've said often in courses and my books, I often learn as much
from my students as I impart. In this case, I discovered that the
reason sales were not meeting the executives' expectations was that
there were no real product managers pushing checking or CDs or
IRAs. Feeling no pressure, the platform people were taking the easy
way out and not really selling product.

So, as I was finishing the branch refresher courses, I went back
to the CEO and told him what I found. I also provided a solution,
suggesting I temporarily take over a product manager role while I
developed people within his organization who could take on the role
permanently. The CEO bought my idea.

As a result, I was imbedded deeper into the organization, and I believe—at least in the CEO's mind—I was perceived as a problem solver, not someone just interested in selling. I'm sure this isn't the last assignment I'm going to get from the bank.

Finally, an oldie from a previous economic downturn: I was hired by a company that manufactured and sold convertible furniture—you know, things like sofa beds. Times were bad, furniture is a big-ticket item, and both showroom traffic and sales were down. The company's manufacturing facility faced layoffs, as did the truckers who delivered the couches, and everyone was pessimistic.

I came in and suggested that the store salespeople stop selling the couches. My idea was that for the short term they concentrate on reupholstering existing furniture. They'd just introduced a new line of fabrics, and I suggested that they start off by contacting customers with convertibles purchased at least five years earlier.

The chances are that their furniture was frayed, and reupholstering was certainly cheaper than buying a new couch. The company bought my idea, which accomplished a number of important goals.

First of all, it increased showroom traffic. People responded to the idea and were reupholstering convertibles. Second, it created a new business, a new profit center, for the company. Third, it increased sales of new convertibles. About 8 percent of the people who came in intending to look at fabrics decided instead to buy new furniture. And as important in the big scheme of things, it enabled the company to retain highly trained and motivated craftsmen whose jobs were threatened by the downturn.

Take Action

1. When you're confronted with a problem with one of your accounts, don't always look at it from the same angle. Try stepping back and thinking as something other than a salesperson. You'll find the solution sometimes jumps out at you.

2. Make a list of four or five accounts that got away from you over the past couple of years. Review each of them and think if there was anything radical or out-of-the-box that you could have suggested to them that might have saved the account.

3. Rethink your relationship with all your clients. How can you get that relationship to move past a simple salesperson-account dichotomy to something else?

Chapter 9

Keep the Basics in Play

One of the ironies of these times is that while the economic world around you is crumbling, the basics of selling remain the same. That is, you will still have to prospect; you will still have to gather sufficient information to come up with a cogent, appealing proposal. And you still will have to give a positive, hopefully energy-filled presentation.

> *The basics of selling*
> *remain the same.*

I have to admit that even I am constantly surprised by how enduring the basics of selling are. I was recently asked to revise and update two of my older books—*Cold Calling Techniques (That Really Work!)* and *Closing Techniques (That Really Work!)*. In both cases I was astonished by how little has changed in the fifteen or so years since I wrote both books. While some of the tools of selling have changed, the fundamentals remain the same.

Since it is possible that you may be unfamiliar with what I consider the basics, let me spend a few minutes summarizing the various facets of selling and how they fit together. My basic philosophy is that selling involves a process—a series of steps. The goal at each step on the highway (except the last, of course) to a signed contract is not the contract itself—but just to get to the next step.

Worrying about making a presentation at a first meeting with a prospect not only makes little sense but also is a distraction. Every step comes in its own time. There's no point in driving yourself around the bend about something that's still on the horizon.

The first thing of course is the cold call. The truth is no one likes to make cold calls. It is a task that almost always ends in failure. And even when it is successful, it doesn't necessarily guarantee that there will be a commission check at the end of the rainbow. But of course it is necessary, because without a flow of new business, the well dries up.

Still, it's not easy to face rejection. So I always advise salespeople to set aside the same time every day to make your cold calls. A friend of mine recently spoke to college and NBA coach Rick Pitino. Pitino says that he schedules tasks he doesn't like to do first thing in the morning when he's fresh. The stuff he likes to do he can do at any time of the day.

It's what I do and recommend. And I don't suggest doing it first thing in the morning when you feel like it, but every day, come hell or high water, until it becomes an ingrained habit.

Step two is going on that first appointment. It is at this stage that you are likely to clarify what I consider are the four essential components of a successful sales process.

1. Are you speaking to the right person? Often enough, sales folks are steered toward lower-level personnel who filter vendors for decision makers. It is obviously key that you determine who the decision maker is, and if it isn't the person you're speaking to, how you get access to him or her.

2. Are you talking about the right product? In your cold call that set up this appointment, you likely told the prospect that you manufacture widgets. He or she might have assumed that you make ten-inch versions when the largest you produce is eight inches. Unless you can produce what the prospect needs, all you are doing is spinning your wheels.

3. Do you have the right price? You don't need to agree on a specific price—that comes later in the process—but you need to know that you're both playing in the same ballpark.

4. Finally, can you deliver on your promise? You need to know that you can fulfill your commitments—that is, get your widgets to the factory when the customer wants them. If your potential client has an immediate need for product while you have a backlog of orders in your pipeline, you may need to pass. Promising something you can't deliver is counterproductive.

If you get past the hurdle of your initial meeting, you've immeasurably improved your odds of at least making it to the finish line—plus you have a shot at winning the race. What's the difference between the two? Information.

Sales Tactic

The key to getting more information is what I've called the Power of Twelve. That is, I tell the prospect that it would really help me make a more intelligent and compelling proposal if I could spend some time with his salespeople and a couple of sales managers. I always attempt to see at least a dozen people besides my initial contact. You don't always get twelve of course, and it takes a lot of extra time. But it is time well invested.

Every person you see gives you another perspective on what the company is currently doing and what its needs are. Because I conduct sales training seminars, my Power of Twelve usually consists of salespeople, their managers, and occasionally some customers. But, depending upon the service or product you sell, you might want to see higher-level executives and people who work on the manufacturing line. The more people you have an opportunity to interact with, the more information you accumulate, and the better your chances of creating a brilliant, irresistible proposal.

The next step is to come up with a proposal that makes sense all around. Before you make a presentation, though, you should first be "righted." By "righted" I mean that you sit down with your contact and go over the information you've gathered and sound him or her out about the direction you're going. This is a good time, too, to find out who will be attending the formal presentation. If it's people you've already been in touch with, you likely have a good idea whether they are on your side—or at least open to your ideas. If the names are new to you, see if there's a way to contact them before the presentation to get a feeling for where they stand.

> *I always attempt to see*
> *at least a dozen people.*

You don't want to wait until you're making a formal presentation to discover that some of the assumptions you've made are misguided or that there are a bunch of influential people you've never met or spoken to aligned against you from the get-go. If you do all these things—and, of course, if you do them correctly—you are as close to a lock as one can be without a signed contract in hand.

The Power of Twelve and presentations will be covered in greater detail in later chapters.

This is only a broad outline of the sales process. (For more details you can consult any one of a couple of dozen books I've written about sales or attend one of my seminars. End of commercial.) But it goes a long way toward explaining what I'll be talking about in the next dozen or so chapters.

Take Action

1. Spend some time reviewing the basics of sales—things like cold calling, closing, and developing prospects. If it helps, read a lot more of my books on those subjects.

2. Set aside an hour each day to do nothing but make cold calls. It doesn't matter if it's in the morning or the afternoon, just as long as it's dedicated to nothing but that.

3. Make a list of all the steps in your sales process. Review that list every couple of weeks and see if you're leaving anything out or spending too much or too little time on any one step.

Chapter 10

Remember: The Rules Have Changed

I've just spent an entire chapter telling you that the basics of selling never change. Now I'm going to spend a chapter telling you how you must change. Clearly when the economy goes to pot, it can't be business as usual.

In normal times, your enemy isn't the competition. You're fighting inertia. But when the economy turns sour, you have additional "enemies." Time becomes a problem. There are just so many hours in a day. In some cases, the media becomes a problem. As noted earlier, if your customers keep reading and hearing about an economic downturn, they start to believe it, even if their business is doing well—and they react accordingly.

You face that problem yourself. It becomes progressively more difficult to put on a happy face when the size of commission checks grows progressively smaller.

In good times there are rare occasions when a prospect is dissatisfied with a current supplier and opens the door to outside competition. Or a company decides to introduce a new product, and invites you in to hear about your offerings.

But as we all know, if we had to wait for these types of opportunities (even in good times) we'd soon be in the poor house. That's why they call us sales reps, not order-taking reps. It's why we earn the big bucks—or at least why we're supposed to.

*Our job is to go out
and find new customers.*

No, our job is to go out and find new customers. And more often than not, these are customers who don't want to be found. They are satisfied with the status quo. By that I mean no one in or around their companies is complaining about the products or services they currently purchase. And as long as there are no complaints, why make changes?

In good or at least better times, you always have a possibility that a prospect will give you a shot. But when times are hard, when people with collars both blue and white are getting laid off left and right, people don't want to stick their necks out of the foxhole. Why take a chance on someone new when someone old isn't causing a problem?

What to do? Over the course of the many books I've written, I've always resisted the temptation to tell readers they need to work harder and smarter. Why? For one thing, they've become such common aphorisms I think they've lost their impact. Have you ever picked up a business book where the author doesn't provide tips on how to work smarter and not harder or work harder and smarter or some variation of hard and smart?

I also felt them obvious. Who doesn't believe that they need to work hard and smart to succeed? However, as I've learned from personal experience, the need for hard work and an intelligent approach to sales is sometimes easy to forget. There have been times of great prosperity when business flowed into my company faster than I could handle it. It made me very happy, very tired, and at times very lazy. So when the difficult times came (as they always do), I was unprepared. And it took me a while to get the company back to where I wanted it to be. And the way I did that was by, yes, working harder and smarter.

Of course, that's easy to say; the difficulty comes in defining what that means. Let me give you a few examples. Consider prospecting. It becomes more necessary than ever to study and understand your ratios. By ratios I mean how many cold calls you have to make to get through to a single prospect. How many prospects do you need to speak to in order to get a single appointment. How many of these first appointments do you generally make that eventually lead to a sale?

Just for the sake of argument, suppose your ratio is fifty cold calls get you ten first appointments. And you garner two sales for every ten first appointments. Your ratio is 50:10:2. In essence, what this boils down to is that every fifty calls you make generate two sales.

However, during knotty economic times, your ratios will likely change. Instead of needing to make fifty calls, you may need to make seventy-five to a hundred cold calls to generate two sales. And that's where working harder comes in.

Sales Tactic

In a previous chapter, I told you to set aside some time every day to make cold calls. Over a couple of weeks, track your success rate and calculate your ratio. You should check this number regularly—every few weeks. Balance it against the state of the economy and the state of your industry. It will tell you a lot about whether you need to change tactics.

If you've been making fifty cold calls a week to earn your income, you may have to put in an extra hour a day on the telephone to maintain your pre-downturn pace. But you won't know that unless you actively keep track of your ratios.

Knowledge Is Power

There are lots of other reasons to keep track of ratios. You need to know them so you can stay on top of your game. Let's suppose that it now takes twenty first appointments to generate one sale. Is it the economy or is it the way you are selling that's caused this discrepancy? It may be nothing but the hard economic times, but you won't know until you examine—or re-examine—the way you sell. And that type of self-awareness is what I consider selling smarter.

In the past, too, I wasn't a proponent of over-researching the companies you cold call. My theory was and remains that the idea isn't to go into a meeting to be a showoff about how much you know concerning the potential client company. The idea is to engage in a conversation of discovery, to get your prospect talking, to get him or her involved in the sales process.

But in difficult times, it is harder to get your foot in the door to initiate that conversation. So you really have to do more research about the company to come up with a way to get in the door. That's working harder.

> *Be more*
>
> *empowered.*

For example, let's suppose you go through some old issues of business publications in your industry and you read a story published a year or so ago that Company X was going to introduce a new greener doodad. You know that it's impossible to make a doodad without your product. But there have been no subsequent reports indicating the company made any progress toward actually manufacturing the new doodad.

Smart selling might be a cold call to check on the status of this project. In a worst-case scenario, the idea was dropped because of the difficulty of introducing a new doodad in bad economic times. That is an opening to point out that your product is perfect for eco-friendly doodads, that the economic times will change, and you'd like to come in for a few minutes, meet him (or her), and discuss this and how else your two companies might work together.

Even if the prospect doesn't agree to see you now, he or she will likely be impressed by your initiative.

In a best-case scenario, the doodad project is still in the works and your timing is perfect. But the extra effort you put into research has enabled you to sell smarter.

Finally, when the selling environment becomes problematic, it is important that you as sales rep be more empowered than you have been in the past. The parameters of what you are allowed to do in terms of price or delivery dates or any of the dozens of other details that can make or break a sale must be enlarged. You may need the authority to give steeper discounts than you were able to previously.

At the very least, the sales process must be streamlined at your firm so that if an offer outside your level of authority can clinch a sale, you need to be able to get an answer within one working day rather than wait for a committee to meet.

In short, you have to become an entrepreneur, not an employee.

Take Action

1. Create a record-keeping system for your ratios. List the cold calls to sales ratio, appointment to sales ratio, prospect to client ratio, and anything else you can think of. You don't need an elaborate system; something on an Excel spreadsheet will do fine.

2. Start a file for information on the companies you cold call. Include newspaper and magazine clippings, information from the web, annual reports, and anything else that might be useful in getting that first appointment.

3. Review the decision-making process at your company. Are there any ways you could streamline it to make things quicker and more efficient?

Chapter 11

Use Your Intelligence

More than any other in this book, I like—nay, love—the title of this chapter. I think the reason is obvious. In all its various meanings, the word "intelligence" encapsulates what I think is important about selling.

I spoke in part about this in the last chapter when I noted that the key to surviving in distressing times is selling smarter—that is, with more intelligence. To do that you have to gather as much information about the client and how he uses your product or service—in short, you have to gather intelligence.

And you have to use that knowledge—the facts, statistics, and data you gather—to make your case in a different manner than you might normally—by using your creative intelligence.

There's another intelligence factor involved. You have to be prepared for every objection a client or potential client can raise. In bad times, buyers have more reasons to say no than ever before. Almost all of the situations I mention below happen during good times as well as bad. It's just that when the economy is failing, it seems they happen more often. Consider the following:

Lower Budgets

Everyone is cutting back. So if you provide a product or service not considered absolutely vital to the company's future, you may be hard hit by bad times. One of the first things many companies cut, for example, is the training budget. The same is true for publicity and advertising and temporary and full-time employment services—among others. But when someone tells me, "Sorry, but my training allocation has been cut," I have to be prepared to make a point that sales training's importance transcends (hopefully) temporary economic setbacks. In fact, a better-trained sales force will better position the company to pull out of the malaise. Almost certainly there is an intelligent argument you can make about your product or service.

Personnel Turnover

Bad times mean layoffs, and your contact at a company is as vulnerable as anyone else. If this is an existing client, you've hopefully already imbedded yourself with others in the company. Also, the new guys (or gals) aren't going to want to make waves fresh out of the starting gate. They'll be too busy getting all their ducks in order. That will give you an opportunity to get to know the replacement and fill him in on your product or service. If the layoff takes place at a company that is not a customer but one you've been working on converting, there is a natural segue: "Ms. Jones, I understand you'll be replacing Bill Smith in the purchasing department. I've been meeting with him for the last couple of months on the possibility of introducing my new widgets into your manufacturing process. What I'd like to do is come in and see you to discuss the status of this project. We were making real progress, and while I don't want to put words in his mouth, I think he agreed this would be a positive step. When would be convenient for you." Of course, before you meet her, you will no doubt gather "intelligence" about Ms. Jones and the kind of person she is. On the other hand, if it is someone with whom you've been unable to get an appointment, the change may actually work in your favor. The new kid on the block may be more receptive than the person she replaced. In fact, the latter's unwillingness to see people may be the reason he was replaced.

Slower Sales of Product/Product Discontinued

The reality is that you don't have much of a comeback if a client tells you the product in which the company used your widgets is being terminated. It's not like you can say, "But I have a quota to meet. Can't you pull the plug six months down the road?" But if you've properly gathered your "intelligence" and seen this coming, you will already have gathered "intelligence" on other products the company manufactures that might benefit from your widgets.

Merger

When two or more companies merge, it generally isn't a merger of equals. One of the companies is generally more equal than the other. You have a better shot at retaining and expanding your business if you've been working with the stronger of the merger partners or if your contact survives "redundancy." In any case, you'll make an effort to see the new person, explain what you've done, why the company bought from you, and what you can bring to the newly combined corporation.

Outsourcing/About to Sign Contract with Competitor at Far Lower Price

In an earlier chapter I mentioned that a former student of mine was faced with a quandary. Facing financial difficulties, one of his best clients was about to buy widgets from an overseas supplier. My student was able: to add value to his company's widgets by doing some assembly for his client; arrange for just-in-time delivery (not always possible from plants located on the other side of the Pacific); and offer guarantees about product quality (not always possible when plants are located on the other side of the Pacific). If price is the main factor, attempt to change the conversation. Talk about quality. It's not necessary to denigrate a particular overseas supplier, but, depending upon your industry, prospects and existing clients may already be aware of tainted products that have been exported from certain countries. Talk about just-in-time delivery. That will save a company money.

Talk about extended payment plans. Talk about your firm's excellent customer service. All these facets of your operation will save your client money, perhaps enough to offset any cost savings from outsourcing. The key is to use your smarts, your intelligence. (And isn't that a great way to end this chapter?)

> *In bad times,*
> *buyers have more reasons to say no.*

Take Action

1. For each of your accounts, note down why the product or service you provide is essential to the well-being of the company. It helps if you can show how the product or service actually helps the account weather bad economic times.

2. List facts about your product or service that go beyond quality; list delivery time, pricing, anything else you can think of. Talk about the product's environmental benefits. In today's world, that's becoming a big consideration.

3. Don't limit your contact with an account to just one person. If possible, get to know others so that if your contact is laid off you have backup.

Chapter 12

Use Time Wisely

We've already spoken about working harder and smarter. By harder, of course, I mean that you need to put in more effort and probably work longer hours than you did before. And by smarter I mean you can't run around aimlessly like that proverbial chicken without a head. Just making (or attempting to make) sales calls on companies that aren't genuine prospects is not only silly and time consuming, it can be demoralizing as well. And again that recurring theme I mentioned (time and again, starting in the introduction) is that it is extremely important to have a positive attitude in negative times.

So the first step is to set priorities. We've already spoken about the most obvious one: existing clients. More so than ever before, you have to pay attention to these companies if for no other reason than that you can't risk losing them. But even more important, existing customers are your best source of new business leads and new business itself.

> *The first step is*
> *to set priorities.*

But let's suppose you have those bases covered. Where do you go next? I'd bet on companies that you've called on in the recent past and just missed signing up. By that I mean you went through the entire sales process, up to and including the presentation, and lost out to a competing company.

I make a number of assumptions here:

1. When you were turned down it was what I call a righteous loss. There was nothing nasty involved; there was no ill will or bruised feelings. You didn't burn any bridges. Someone else made a proposal that the company preferred more than yours.

2. You made an effort to find out what was wrong with your proposal. Was it just price? Was it quality? Was it customer service? But to the extent possible, you have a good idea of where you went astray.

3, You left the door open to come back. You told your contact you planned to stay in touch (and you did) with the idea of revisiting the situation in six months.

4. You let yourself soar. That is, now you have ideas different from (and better than) your original presentation to discuss with the prospect. You need to be able to make a case for what you are able to do that the existing vendor can't or doesn't do. You need to be able to illustrate why the company should switch to you at a time when most companies—and most personnel—are reluctant to make any changes.

5. You've done research. It assumes that in the six or nine months since your presentation, you've followed the company and the industry. By that I mean more than just reading the consumer and trade press (although that's certainly important); you also need to stay in touch with your primary contact as well as others you met during your initial sales process. Regular contact may enable you to find out potential openings for you. These contacts may not come out and say they're dissatisfied with your competition, but they may offer little hints that the company is not getting the service it was promised, that deliveries aren't coming in on time, that customer service is lacking. It will provide a direction for you when you attempt to revisit the possibility of coming aboard as a supplier.

If you examine the five steps I mentioned above you'll see I believe that this is the kind of stuff you should be doing on a daily basis no matter the state of the economy. This is true. Then why make a point of it now? Simply: while everyone should be doing these things, very few people do them when the economy is good.

When you're raking in the dough and the commissions, why bother? Some of these steps require extra work. Why spend time trying to come up with an innovative approach to a prospect who already turned down what was your best shot when there are so many other orders to fill? Why spend time reading about and studying a company that said "no" once. Why take a prospect to lunch who already has demonstrated the inability to see your wisdom?

Because at some point you're going to have the time. The bubble always bursts. What goes up must come down. Do you care to read any more platitudes? The bottom line is that it's just smart business. If you've gone through the sales process in the correct way, you know the company and you likely know many of its key decision-making employees. That makes you wiser. The other significant point is that they are using your product or service; they're just not buying it from you.

Sales Tactic

Once every four to six months, call your contacts at those companies where you tried and failed to make a sale. Stay in touch with them, keep your name in front of them. As things change, there will be more opportunities to go back to them with your products. And if you truly soar, you may come up with some ideas for improving their business that will knock their socks off.

You know the players and how they think. You have an idea where you went wrong in your proposal and perhaps, if you've stayed in touch, what the incumbent is doing incorrectly now. So it's a simple phone call to the prospect to say:

"Bob, a lot has changed in the six months since I made my presentation. I've thought this through and made a number of changes in my presentation. I've tried to take into account those areas where I may have made a misstep the last time around and also the way the economy looks at least for the short term. I think I may have come up with a couple of ideas that I believe you'll find quite attractive."

So if you have not been doing this, take out laptop (or paper and pen) and try to come up with at least a half dozen or so companies who meet the standards I've outlined. And then Google them. Get your hands on every bit of information about what's going on with them since your presentations. Check back issues of trade magazines in the field. Many have archives on line. And search for a way to reintroduce yourself to the mix.

Make this your number one priority. Priority number two should be people who once did business with you but stopped for a "legitimate" reason: another supplier was able to offer better terms, went to overseas sourcing, slowed production of the product you were involved in.

> *Search for a way*
> *to reintroduce yourself.*

Why stay in touch? Why go there? Pretty much for the same reasons you'd want to revisit clients who almost signed a deal with you. You know the company. They know you. And it should be relatively easy to re-establish contact there.

CASE IN POINT

A consultant I know who teaches business writing taught his course at a small advertising agency. He ran two sessions a year, one in the spring and one in the fall for the company's account executives for about five years running. Then he got a call from the HR manager that the agency was dropping the course.

He asked, but no, it wasn't anything he did wrong. On the contrary, it was something he did right. The people who'd taken his course were doing extremely well. They'd simply run out of people who needed his training. There wasn't a lot of money involved in the Big Scheme of things, but it was enough to annoy him. And, in any event, no one likes to lose a client.

My friend left on amicable terms but stewed privately for a little while. He was determined to win the account back. It took a few months, but eventually he came up with a brand extension idea I think ingenious. He created a basic grammar/introduction to writing course for lower-level people, administrative assistants and the like. It's a much-needed product. The agency signed him up, and the courses were quickly and completely filled when they were announced. As important, this course created a stream of students for his business-writing course.

This happened because my friend didn't burn any bridges when he left. He knew people at the agency, a couple of whom had complained about the nonprofessional quality of their assistants' writing, and he was able to put one and one together and come up with three. ✦

I've had my own experiences with going back to accounts. I'd worked for years at a large international insurance company. I got along with everyone. But, as sometimes (actually too often) happens, the company brought in a training manager who had a different philosophy about sales training from mine. He also had a trainer he'd worked with in a different industry whom he was determined to bring in.

I did pretty much everything I could to keep his account, which generated a lot of bucks. I made several trips to the head office in Europe, but when push came to shove (and correctly so) the corporate-level executives decided they were going to go with their manager's choice.

I stayed in touch with everyone I knew there, including the new training director who canned me. Every once in a while, I'd find a reason to drop them a line. Every time one of my books came out I'd send out autographed copies, just so they'd know I was still here.

Fortunately (for me), the new sales trainer that was brought in was not sufficiently versed in the insurance business. The people put through the course were not giving him the same high evaluations I'd consistently received. And my guess is that the insurance company was not entirely satisfied with the performance of the course's graduates, either.

About two years after I was replaced, I got a call from the training director to see if I'd be interested in giving some of my classes again at a regional level. I did. The classes went well and my schedule with the company continues to expand.

The company in this case wasn't influenced by bad economic times. But the story illustrates a couple of important points:

If you lose an account, bite your tongue. You can never tell what the future holds—including the possibility of more business from this same company.

It stands to reason that you have a better shot at picking up business at a place where you are a known commodity than starting fresh from a cold call.

When business is bad, you have to take a military approach. Time is precious. Pick out and concentrate on high priority targets.

Take Action

1. Keep in regular contact with companies where you failed to make a sale.

2. Maintain regular sources of information about those companies; use the web, the news media, and every possible source to see if an opportunity has opened up for you to revisit them with your product or service.

3. Never burn bridges. As a sales professional, you're all about building them, not destroying them. And if you think you rubbed someone at a company the wrong way, find out what you did and fix it.

Chapter 13

Get Over the Peaks and Through the Valleys

Peaks and valleys are a regular part of the sales rep's condition—never more so than when times are bad. There's really no way to avoid them, but you can smooth things a bit by understanding your ratios. I've already discussed the importance of this. Now I'd like to give you a practical example of how ratios can be used.

Let us, for example, assume that sales rep Sally has twenty active prospects and that over time she discovered that twenty potential clients is just about the right figure for her. If she has any more than that going at one time, it is too many to handle. Any fewer than that and Sally's commission checks seem to get smaller.

Further, let us say her closing ratio is one in five; that is, for every five potential closers she's pursuing, one will actually sign a contract. Finally, let me suppose that Sally signs one prospect.

The conventional wisdom is that Sally has to cold call until she finds another prospect to replace the one she signed. But as so often happens, the conventional wisdom is wrong. If her ratios are to be believed, the moment she signed one contract, there were four others among her prospects likely to turn her down. So, in order to replace that one signed client, she really has to come up with five more prospects.

I know this sounds a little counterintuitive, like a kind of mathematical legerdemain. Let me try to explain it in terms of flipping coins. Every time you flip a coin the odds are fifty-fifty that it will turn up heads and fifty-fifty that it show tails. The odds remain constant, fifty-fifty, even if that coin has shown up heads ten times in a row. But at the end of a year of coin flipping, heads will have appeared roughly half the time and tails the other half.

It's the same with your sales ratio. You may say, "Steve, just because I signed one client on doesn't mean I'm not going to sign the next one and the one after that."

And you're absolutely right. Like the coin that keeps coming up heads, you can have a peak week or a month where your prospects find you and your company irresistible, where no one can say no to you. But ultimately the averages come into play, and the chances are your ratio will hover around one closing for every five prospects.

So at some point, you're likely to get a bunch of refusals in a row and find yourself in a valley so deep you don't know how, when, or if you'll be able to scale the next hill. And the odds of that happening drastically increase in an economic downturn.

I understand if every time you close a deal you pause to do a celebratory lap around the office figuring you have time to replace one prospect. But what Sally has to do is start looking for five prospects, so she'll have potentially peak possibilities when a valley seems just over the horizon.

The critical point here is the risk involved in not keeping your supply line open. We all have a tendency to get lazy when times are good. If you're on the verge of signing four contracts, who needs to spend a lot of time cold calling?

YOU DO!

> *It's hazardous to*
> *forget your ratios.*

Even in the best of times, it's hazardous to forget your ratios and the constant need to replenish your supply lines. You and I both know that you're not always going to be able to replace each sale with five new prospects (or however many you need according to your ratio), but that always ought to be your goal.

If you can do that, you can smooth out not only the peaks and valleys of your normal career, but be better positioned to survive when the economy hits the tank.

Ingredients for Success in Bad Times

There are very few advantages of being older. In fact, the only one that comes to mind right now is that you've built a storehouse of life experiences. And if you're intelligent, you will use those life lessons.

As I write this, the world is going through a major financial crisis. Major companies are on the brink of failure, unemployment is reaching record levels, and the future seems bleak.

> *You've built a storehouse of life experiences.*
> *And . . . you will use those life lessons.*

But it's been this way before. I lived through an economic crisis where inflation hovered near 20 percent and that was roughly the mortgage rate, too. I've seen times so bad that they put wage price controls into effect. When there were no jobs to be had. When other bubbles burst. I lived through 9/11.

And looking back, I remember how depressed I got. Long-standing clients were cutting back. It seemed impossible to make a successful cold call. But I survived and ultimately prepared myself for prosperity.

As I already have at several points in this book—and will do again—I'm going to talk about a change in attitude. And I'm not sure how best to do it without making it sound phony. Look, if someone says to you the key to success is putting on a happy face, what does that mean? When you are facing a wall of "Thanks, but no thanks" day after day, how do you put on a happy face? How do you read about putting on a happy face without saying to yourself, "this is baloney, psychobabble"? How do you change your personality, your approach to sales?

I understand that. But for the moment, suspend disbelief. Suppose that putting on a happy face really could increase your sales. Well, then no doubt you would smile all the time. You'd start every day reminding yourself the importance of happy face. And if you caught a glimpse of yourself in the mirror and you were frowning, you would turn that frown around, wouldn't you?

I firmly believe that some of the hints I provide below will increase your sales in bad times. If nothing else, they will make you stand out from the crowd (unless the crowd also reads this book). So I ask you to do two things. First of all, suspend disbelief. This will make a difference.

Second, write down the following paragraphs on a piece of paper you look at every morning, before every cold call and before every appointment. Do that all the time and eventually it will be come second nature to you, a habit.

What I am going to suggest in the following paragraphs is really simple, but can be life changing. When I went through economic crises in the past and when my business was going down the tubes along with the economy, I called a time-out. I did exactly the things I've suggested you do: I created a business plan for myself. I looked at where I wanted to go and examined whether the road I was taking would get me there. It turned out since I'd last examined the plan, the economy had created a series of super-highways and I was still on the service road. Only now, with the economy down, the highway was empty.

CASE IN POINT

Before, I'd concentrated on selling my courses to small and medium-size companies. I felt that many conglomerates might think my then one-person shop was too small for them, incapable of servicing sprawling empires around the country.

My first epiphany was that the conglomerates were frequently made up of perhaps dozens of companies that were not much bigger than the companies I was already targeting. Moreover, the prospects here were more valuable than any I'd approached previously. A good program or series of programs here might lead to additional business not only at that company but also by referral, at sister companies in the corporation.

I also realized that what I had conceived of as a negative could actually be turned around. When I went into a large national company that required sales training at multiple locations, I frequently was told my company was too small. They said they preferred to deal with training companies that had multiple locations. They felt it was cheaper and courses could be scheduled much more rapidly than if they had to wait for me to fit them in.

My response was I was worth waiting for. I created my courses from my personal experiences. I believed in it. I delivered it with the conviction of an entrepreneur who understood that his livelihood depended on every class being great. For that reason, I refused to use facilitators—that is, stand-in teachers—and taught everything myself.

Finally, I told them, while it's all well and good to train your sales force when times are good, this was the time they needed a boost. This was the time they needed to be exposed to other methods. This was the time they'd likely be most receptive to change.

Not everyone bought in to my argument, but enough did that my business started to improve despite red ink flowing elsewhere. The same can happen to you. ✦

It starts here:

This is a time to find a vision for yourself. It is a time to reinvent who you are. It is like moving to a new town and changing schools. You have no history. If bullies picked on you, well you left them behind. People (and companies) are falling left and right, and you're still there. That's good, because it means there's more room for you. The super-highway is all yours, and you can make yourself into anything you want to be.

You need to establish ownership of your own future. Many of us tend to go through our professional sales lives with a sense of dread. We're always afraid to offend. And rather than offer something new and risk offending a client, we tend to fall back on the same old same old. But if you take ownership, you have the choice to go off into a new direction. Choice? When times are bad and no one is buying, what choice do you really have?

As noted previously, *this is an opportunity to be creative.* Ask yourself what can you bring to the buyers' tables that they haven't seen, heard, or considered before. I'll bet that there are innovative ideas you've harbored but were previously afraid to articulate because you didn't want to rock the boat. Hey, people, the boat is sinking. We're open to any ideas you might have. By ideas, of course, we mean a way that can help your clients do what they do better than they currently are. You know your product. You (should) know their company. How can your product be better for their needs and desires? Is there a different way to explain it or illustrate it? I bet there is.

If, as I hope, you buy into this, it's important to remember that you must do more than just read this chapter and close the book.

You have to post this advice somewhere that you'll see it every day as a reminder of the changes you need to make. You need to practice these changes until they become natural to you, a habit. And if you do, not only will you survive every downturn, every dark valley, but you will prosper, too, when you start to climb a peak as the economy gets back on an upswing.

Take Action

1. Write down on a piece of paper where you want to be in five years—in your career, your life, everything. Then start thinking of what it will take to get you there. And no excuses. This is the first step toward taking ownership of your life.

2. Sit down with a couple of colleagues—maybe even try this with clients you've worked with a lot—and start throwing out ideas for what to do in the economic downturn. Sure, a lot of them will be silly or won't work. But out of this collective brainstorming, some pretty good things can come.

3. Follow Sally's example: when every time you close one deal, try to replace it with five prospects.

Chapter 14

Find Out What They're Really Saying

In the avalanche of self-pity we, as sales reps, feel when the economy and our commissions take a nosedive, we tend to forget that we're not alone.

Many of our clients and prospects also feel a measure of jeopardy. If you were the purchasing manager for a stock brokerage firm or bank or automotive manufacturer, would you feel secure? I don't think so. And that of courses changes the way they are likely to react to you and others.

Obviously, listening, paying attention to both verbal and nonverbal clues, is a natural part of any relationship—especially so in sales. But it becomes even more important in difficult economic times.

Consider this: You've developed a very good relationship with Jack, the vice president of purchasing for a billion-dollar corporation. You've gone out together socially, your families exchange holiday cards, and you believe his account is the closest thing you have to an annuity.

But suddenly Jack doesn't return your calls as quickly as he once did. When you visit his office, things are a little off. He is not as quick to laugh at your jokes. He moves the conversation in a different direction when you want to talk about the future. Clearly something is up.

It may be nothing to do with your business relationship; perhaps Jack is having problems at home. Or it could be that cutbacks at his company have forced him to take on more responsibility—and he's feeling the pressure. But are you willing to take a chance that your account is unrelated to Jack's change of behavior? If so, ignore it and make believe nothing has happened. But my inclination would be to pay attention.

In the real world, the transformation of Jack's behavior might very well affect you. There are any number of reasons why. But the likelihood is that change is in store and that you may be the odd man (or woman) out.

Frankly, I've been in this situation myself, and I can tell you from practical experience what doesn't work. And that is putting your head in the sand and ignoring all the signs pointing to bad news in your future.

Sales Tactic

If you're faced with a client like Jack, you can't ignore things. Talk to him, ask him out for a drink, but get him talking. And listen. The listening part's really important.

When he tells you what the problem is, and if he suggests that he can no longer use your services or products, that's your chance to soar—to counter his arguments and come up with some solution that's so breathtaking it'll . . . well, take his breath away.

A few years ago, Richard, my contact at a major client, started acting differently, almost strangely. I always called on him in early October to discuss renewing my contract. For the previous eight to ten years, this was virtually a scripted meeting. We'd go to lunch, we'd take out our calendars and work out the best dates for the following year. Our relationship was such that if I was booked or holding a date that he wanted, he'd graciously ask, "Okay, what do you have available around this time?"

But this go-around, he postponed setting dates. We're not ready yet, he told me. And he kept putting it off until late December. Finally, I received a letter from him the last week of the year, between Christmas and New Years, saying the company was not going to renew my contract.

I called Rich immediately, of course, but he was away on vacation. When I finally got ahold of him, he apologized for not letting me know sooner. He said he liked my sales courses and had spent the last quarter of the year trying to save my business with the firm. When he couldn't, he was ashamed to tell me in person; that's why he sent me the letter.

My first reaction was anger. I thought he handled the situation in cowardly manner. I felt we'd known each other and done business together long enough that I deserved to be told in person.

I was even more upset when I found out what happened. A large training company provided a variety of courses at my friend's firm. It was expanding into sales training as well and convinced the senior vice president of human resources that there were advantages to dealing with one company:

- Administrative costs would be lower, since there'd be only one contract to work on.
- Personnel costs would be reduced by dealing with one supplier.
- By signing an additional series of courses with the company, there'd be volume cost savings on all the courses the company provides.

If I had learned about this earlier, I might have been able to turn things around. My argument in this case is if you have heart problems, you don't go to a general practitioner. You make sure you're treated by the best cardiologist around. It's the same with training. If you want to improve your sales force, do you see the same company teaching your administrative assistants how to send out memos? No, of course not. You go to a specialist. That's the argument I would have made.

Frankly, in a worst-case scenario, I probably would have worked something out financially. After all, this was a big account.

But the more I thought about it, the less angry I became—at least at my contact. I understand that no one wants to deliver bad news, especially to someone with whom you have a relationship. Moreover, he genuinely tried to save the business for me. The real problem was that while he didn't use words, he did try to tell me that something was up, and I refused to get it.

It isn't that I didn't notice. I kept putting it off for a couple of reasons. I suspected there was bad news, and I didn't want to hear it. As long as I wasn't told that I had lost the account, I still had the account. But I also knew Rich was reluctant to tell me something, and I didn't want to back him into a corner. If I had, however, there might have been a major difference in my financial results the following year. At the very least, had I found out in sufficient time, I might have concentrated more on getting new business.

> *Prospects . . . may face a change of*
> *circumstances that they are*
> *reluctant to tell you about.*

And it isn't just long-time clients who evade straight answers. Prospects who've been encouraging to you may face a change of circumstances that they are reluctant to tell you about. It's got to be a blow to their ego to, say, be stripped of buying power and now need to go to a higher authority for approval on purchases they routinely signed up for.

One of the main themes of this (and quite frankly all my books) is that information is key. Getting the straight dope—even if you don't like what you hear—is important. Knowing what's going on won't necessarily get you a new account or save an old one, but at the very least it allows you react. It gives you a shot.

I've gotten a number of phone calls lately from sales reps all complaining about how tough the economy is. When I ask, "What are you doing about it?" they reply, "What can you do?" In short, they're not doing anything differently now than they've done before. And in a few cases, they've actually stopped selling.

Sales reps have to revise their approach and be far more flexible and creative. They need to listen with a jaundiced ear. That is, when a client says they've temporarily put your project on hold, the word "temporary" may just be thrown in as an afterthought.

What that likely means is that the company—like pretty much every other company out there—is in a cash bind and won't be doing business with you any time soon. Here's where your flexibility may come in.

Information

is key.

Work out with your management ways you can save clients money. Perhaps spreading out payments or delayed billing is all that's needed to solve the problem. The economy is the eight-hundred-pound gorilla in the room. Bring it up. Understand your clients' pain. Show that you may be the analgesic that makes the pain go away.

Admit that things are different, and listen to what your customer says. And then figure out what he means.

Take Action

1. If an account rep starts to act squirrelly, don't just ignore it. Probe to find out what's going on. The earlier you get her or him to tell you the scoop, the more time you have to do something about it.

2. Search for a variety of solutions and talk them over with the rep. Remember—you want to act like an entrepreneur, not just a salesperson.

3. Be flexible and creative. And listen. I can't repeat that enough.

Chapter 15

Network

I've learned much of what I know by making mistakes. One of my best learning experiences ever happened like this.

I was young and had been in my own business for just a few years. As a matter of course I joined a training trade association; I figured that was a good way to get my name known. In fact, I soon became active in the local chapter, joined a committee, and was even named Member of the Month for my activities.

But I noticed a couple of things at the meetings I attended. First, most of the people who came were consultants like me—people interested in selling their wares not buying mine. And the few human resources and training people who were there described themselves as being "in transition." By "in transition," of course, they meant they were looking for work in the same way I was looking for business.

After a year or so with nothing to show for it, I lowered my profile. (I realize this statement makes me sound more mercenary than I really want to publicly admit. But while I'm sure some people joined the association for the greater betterment of the training industry, I wasn't one of them. I had a business I wanted to grow, and I was in the association for the betterment of my family.)

I didn't quit but didn't do any extra volunteer work. I attended meetings sporadically and then dropped out entirely. A couple of years later, I started attending meetings again and was introduced to the training manager for an extremely large communications company. We started talking, and I told her what I did. I (diplomatically) asked her if she had any sales training needs.

For the record, when we were introduced I didn't just say, "Hi, my name is Steve Schiffman and I do sales training. Can I sell you anything?" We were standing at a mini bar the organization sets up in the room during the networking pre-dinner phase of the meeting. The conversation took place over twenty or so minutes and was handled extremely tactfully. What do you people think of me, anyway? But I digress.

It turned out she didn't need sales training at the company. In fact, she'd just hired someone. Perhaps I knew him. She told me his name and added, "He's very active in the association." In fact, she didn't really know whom to hire, but she knew this gentleman through their work at the training group and signed him up.

"I guess it was bad timing," she said when I told her my history with the organization. "It just goes to show you how important visibility is."

This is a lesson I've never forgotten. It raises the philosophical question: if you offer the best product in the woods, and no one knows about it, is it really the best product? Or something like that. You get the point. And I think we can all agree that networking has huge importance at any time. But it takes on a greater urgency when times are bad.

As we've noted in previous chapters, when the economic situation deteriorates, companies are reluctant to make any changes. Changes involve risks, and people who do the risk dance sometimes have to pay to the piper with their jobs. If you were the purchasing manager of a company facing hard times, would you willingly bring in a new supplier—especially if no one is complaining about the old one? You might get a better price, but quality may be inferior, or service or any one of a dozen things that ultimately can cost someone a job. And if you're not planning to change suppliers, why bother seeing competitors?

Networking has huge importance at any time.
But it takes on greater urgency when times are bad.

The reality, though, is that people do change suppliers all the time. They may do it for different reasons in good times (to get better quality) than in bad times (to get a better price). But if you are not visible, you won't have a shot. And one of the best ways to gain visibility is to network.

Some people are better at it than others. I know one consultant who insists that his work should stand on its own. Build a field of good work and clients will come. Well it doesn't happen that way. Good work, like the trees that fall in the forest unnoticed, doesn't mean anything if no one is aware of it.

Sales Tactic

What are the professional organizations in the industry you sell into? Where do they hold their conventions? How often? Make it your business to find out the answers to these questions.

There are many avenues for networking, and the computer age has made it easier to connect. There are no secrets here. All you need to do is recognize how important networking is—particularly in hard economic times—and make an effort. For example, you probably have between one hundred and two hundred acquaintances.

Do they know what you do? Do you know what they do? Are there places where your business interests intersect and you can help each other? Find out. It's pretty basic stuff.

When anyone asks me what I do I give them the whole story, including what I've done and how I've done it. Who knows if they can help me—or if they know someone who can.

I carry business cards wherever I go, and I'm not afraid to use them. There was a time I thought handing them out was a little pretentious, but my attitude about that has changed. There are times now I'm tempted to place them under the windshield wiper of every car I pass. I've found that people forget names quicker than they forget conversations. They may not remember the name Steve Schiffman, but they won't forget they met a sales trainer. "What was his name again? Wait, I think I have his card."

I carry business cards wherever I go.

Join every association that makes sense and a few that may not immediately come to mind. If there is an AAWSR—or American Association of Widget Sales Reps—join it. If your widgets are used in the manufacture of airplanes or cars, join the AAAM the American Association of Airplane (Automobile) Manufacturers. Get active. Be visible. Don't make the same mistake I did.

Don't limit yourself to the obvious organizations. Join the local chamber of commerce. Become an Elk or a Mason. And don't forget your alumni association. Who knows where catching up with former classmates will lead you.

There are numerous business social networking sites on the web. Join. There's no charge. And if nothing else, it will show friends and potential clients that you are at the forefront of technology.

Make yourself available to give speeches or appear as part of an industry panel at a meeting or convention. No one knows your product line as well as you, and there's no reason you shouldn't flaunt it. I generally give one or two speeches a month, and by my guess 10 percent of the audience will approach me immediately and tell me, "What you said makes sense. You can help my company." More people will contact me later when they return to their offices to say the same thing. Obviously this doesn't all lead to sales—at least right away—but these are all potential cold calls that will be answered.

Don't be shy about promoting yourself. Get articles published in industry papers. If you're a good writer, write them yourself. If not, have your company public relations person help.

Become active in your community. Coach your kids' soccer teams. Get appointed to the local tree-planting committee. Become an officer in your church or synagogue. It will help you get to heaven, and maybe get you some business while you're still here on Earth.

Take Action

1. Make a list of the most important five organizations in your industry and join at least three of them.

2. Set aside the time to attend the conventions of two or three professional organizations. And bring lots of business cards to pass out.

3. Join one or more electronic networks such as LinkedIn. These sites are becoming more popular all the time as places where professionals can meet online.

Chapter 16

Deal with Your Manager

Let us call to mind, for a moment, your sales manager, a person so helpful as to make a saint seem mean spirited. He guides you on every sale without interfering. She provides every type of support material you ask for. He blocks out dunderhead corporate executives who seem intent on sabotaging your best efforts.

Yes, let us imagine this sales manager. And then let us awake from our reverie and get back to the real world. There probably are sales managers like that, but I never worked for one. I've come reasonably close a couple of times, but, as they say, close only counts in horseshoes.

There are a number of reasons that sales managers don't always operate the way those of us on the firing line would like. The most obvious is they are not managers. Managing is hard. I've met a few and worked with (though sadly not for) several really great managers. I don't think you can learn people skills; I've come to believe that the ability to motivate people the way they do is genetic.

Very often successful salespeople are offered management jobs. But success in one area is not necessarily transferable to another. Or people come in from another industry, are unfamiliar with the way you traditionally work, and don't care to learn. Or they're stubborn, opinionated, and/or not very nice.

Sure, those types of managers are counterproductive, but when times are good you work around them. When people are buying, who needs a sales manager? Of course, the opposite is true, as well. When times are bad, you need to be able to work with your sales manager.

First, there's something you have to keep in mind. Your managers are facing a great deal of pressure to produce. Their jobs may be on the line. To make things better, they not only have to service you, but all your colleagues as well. You need to be wise in the way you use them.

And there is something managers need to keep in mind: Their success is contingent upon your success, and they better find the time to help you.

> *Your managers are facing a great*
> *deal of pressure to produce.*

In short, unless you come to a meeting of the minds, success may prove elusive for the both of you. Especially in bad times, neither of you will be successful if your relationship is adversarial. Here are some suggestions on issues that need to be resolved:

Speak the Same Language

Although I understand the rationale for them, I'm not a big fan of call reports. They are often a colossal waste of time better spent selling. I've reviewed hundreds, probably thousands of call reports. The biggest problem I find is that many are filled with meaningless jargon or catch-all phrases written just so the rep can have something down on paper (or software) and tell the boss, yes, I finished my call reports. Writing things like, "I have things under control here" or "Planning another appointment" is meaningless and is a practice you need to stop. Both of you—the rep and the manager—have to stop talking in circles. Avoid jargon. Be clear about what's going on, because if the two of you cannot communicate effectively, it will hinder your ability to get your message across to the prospect or client. Again, I'm not a fan of call reports, but as long as you have to sit down and write, do them correctly. They will help you remember the particulars of a call and will better enable your manager to provide assistance.

Be Honest

If a sale isn't working out or you see that you are on the verge of losing a longtime client, let your manager know. Keeping it a secret doesn't mean he or she won't find out; it will only delay the inevitable. On the other hand, if the manager is informed early on, he might be able to come up with a plan to salvage the situation. Beyond that, however, you need to build trust between the two of you. When times are bad, you as the sales rep who is out in the field need to have more flexibility than you do in better times. You may need to make decisions in the field that used to be above your pay grade. What manager will cede that authority to someone he or she doesn't trust? If you can forge a positive, trusting relationship, a manager can work wonders for you. She can come with you to visit a client, adding a level of gravitas and urgency to a call the prospect or client is likely to feel complimented by. The manager serves as a conduit between you and the Big Bosses. You may want or need something that requires a higher level of approval. Again if she trusts you, she'll go to bat for you.

Be Entrepreneurial

Take control of your sales life by using all the tools you have available—including your manager. Do you need new pricing or billing? See the manager, explain what you need and why you need it, and push him to push your needs to the appropriate authorities. Are clients complaining about the lack of good customer support for your product? In better times a manager might avoid an internal political squabble and not mention the problem. But in bad times that can't happen—and because you've built a level of trust, it won't need to. Critically examine your sales material—the brochures and samples you use on a daily basis. If they're boring to you, they may be as boring to your customers. That's right. Go to your manager and see if he can get the marketing department to redo the tired material.

Willingness to seek help will likely build your relationship with your manager.

...ager's Wisdom

...l managers are wise. But some are. If you run into
...where you need advice, ask. A lot of sales reps don't, fear-
ing that questions come across as a sign of weakness. I beg to differ.
I think asking questions is a sign of confidence in your own abilities.
You're okay with asking for help if you're having a problem. Also, your
willingness to seek help will likely help build your relationship with
the manager.

Don't Stop Learning

When times are bad, one of the first things to go down the tubes is a
company's training budget. But tight times are exactly when you need
the competitive edge that training can provide.

Work Within the System

Sales more than other professions, I think, attracts go-it-aloners, mav-
ericks who consider themselves road warriors. But in bad times, you
can't be an army of one. That doesn't mean you have to stifle your
creativity. On the contrary. Creativity is encouraged. By that I mean
creativity within the system. If you're the guy who refuses to do call
reports or gets them in haphazardly, mend your ways. Play ball. Don't
be—and professional basketball fans will appreciate this—Stephon
Marbury. One rotten apple can spoil the team.

Take Action

1. Make sure you've got regularly scheduled meetings with your
manager—whether they're once a week, once a month, or once a
quarter. If you can't have a face-to-face sit-down, spend some time on
the phone together.

2. Reread some of your old call reports, trying as much as possible
to look at them with a fresh eye. Circle all the general, jargony, meaningless phrases and make a personal vow never to use them again.

3. When you talk to your manager, always try to ask at least one
question and listen—that's right, listen—to the answer you get.

Chapter 17

Independent Reps

Independent reps are hired by companies to sell goods or services, usually in territories where it doesn't make economic sense to field their own sales force. Most often, reps specialize in a particular field—let's say plumbing supplies. They may carry a line of pipes from one company, wrenches from another, those little torchy things plumbers use from a third.

Individually, those lines are generally not enough to make a living on in this territory, but collectively, since the independent rep usually calls on the same clients for all his lines, he or she can make a nice income.

But even in the best of times, it's a difficult way to make a living. Independent reps lead an entrepreneurial life. Unlike many if not most salespeople, they (I'm talking about the partners) live entirely off of commissions. They pay their own expenses. And, irony of ironies, if they build the business of one of their suppliers up to a respectable level, the supplier will often come and put one of his own salespeople in the territory—or insist that your commission structure be renegotiated, downward, of course.

Moreover, the most successful independent reps often have less input—about promotional material, about pricing, about product—than the lowliest sales assistant on the supplier's headquarters staff.

It doesn't sound like a great deal, does it? But the truth is it can be a great life for some people—especially the classic, independent-minded road warrior. Depending upon your lines and territory, you can make a lot of money. Especially when times are good.

But what to do in bad times if you're an independent rep? Depending on how you structure your company, you likely will be able to draw some money against future commissions, but there ain't no pot of gold at the end of that rainbow. However, there are a number of ways that you can either protect or insulate yourself.

> *Don't lose confidence.*
>
> *You are not easily replaceable.*

First and foremost, *don't lose confidence.* You are not easily replaceable. What? Does your manager leave headquarters once a year for a drive-by with you? He doesn't know your clients. He doesn't know their needs. And he doesn't know the way you service them. Unless you are making so much in commissions from him that you can be replaced by a regional office, a secretary, and a salesperson, he's not likely to mess with you. And even then you're still in a stronger bargaining position than HQ staffers—who draw salary, benefits, and vacation days. Moreover, my experience with independent reps is that they have a closer personal relationship with their clients than salaried reps do. I attribute this to the fact that they carry so many lines; each sales call is longer than the perfunctory half hour from a salaried salesperson with only a single product to sell

Don't cut back, either. With sales down, you may be tempted to cut back on client visits and sales trips around your territory. Resist that temptation. Now more than ever is the time for you to squeeze every spare nickel out of existing clients and to beat the bushes for new prospects.

Sales Tactic

There are other areas ripe for cutbacks. Stay at less expensive hotels. Don't eat in the hotel coffee shop (where a glass of juice is $6) when there's a cheaper diner just up the block. In fact, cut back everything except your selling effort.

I know. You work hard and you don't want to scrimp on yourself. But things are different in a downturn. So you're going to have to make some adjustments. Frankly, I don't care where you cut back—so long as it isn't on selling.

Trade shows are one place where you might be able to make some good inroads. They're important not only for networking with existing and potentially new customers, but also for finding new lines to carry. In fact, if in the past you've gone primarily to regional shows in your territory, go to national shows. That's where the suppliers' corporate biggies are and where you'll make contacts to add news lines—or replace existing ones.

If you've been doing a good job in your territory, the chances are that area plumbing supply suppliers know who you are. With the economy in shambles, now is the time to make a case for your business. If they have sales forces in the area, going independent can save them money. It sounds cruel, but in the face of decreasing market share, what executive wants to continue to pay salary plus commission plus health care when she can save thousands annually by signing on with you? You're a sales rep. Sell yourself.

> *If, in the past, you've gone to regional shows, go to national shows.*

Don't get paranoid, but . . . if General Motors can go under—and it is not as far-fetched as it might have been a few years ago—so can the suppliers whose lines you carry. You don't want to be caught short. If one of your suppliers goes under, leaving a bunch of your customers hanging—well that doesn't reflect well on you. And it will affect your other lines. Let's say I order some pipe from you and before I receive it the company goes out of business. Well, that delays the project I'm working on and reduces my level of trust in you. So not only am I not going to order pipe from you anymore, I'm not going to order anything from you. Remember, a lot of your relationship with me and your other clients is key to your success—and trust is an important part of that relationship. If you suspect trouble, attend national shows.

Get the home office involved. Ask the sales manager who visits you just once a year to come out more often and for longer periods of time. Take him on sales calls with you—and don't worry about the other lines you carry. If you bring the sales manager for ABC Pipe with you, your customers are probably not going to bring up DEF Wrenches. And it makes no difference even if they do. Certainly she knows you represent other products besides hers. The point is that she has to see what your customers are saying—good and bad. At the very least she'll see you're putting in the effort. And in a best-case scenario, her visit may provide her with clues on how best to help not only you but her direct reports, as well.

Stay open to new ideas. I know it's difficult to take time off to attend sales seminars or courses. If you're not out selling, you're not making money. Bu the same rules that apply to salaried sales staff apply to you as well. In this economy, there's not much activity. What better time to go out and take a course? When you visit clients, don't make it all about selling. Make it about gaining wisdom. Ask about what's going on in the business. Perhaps the client has been approached by someone else with an innovative idea you can adapt and adopt for your own business. Seek out your peers at the trade shows you now attend to see if you can pick up tips.

Remember that this, too, shall pass. Eventually business will improve. How well you do then depends a lot upon what you do now and how well you build for the future.

Take Action

1. Make a list of four or five trade shows you haven't attended and plan to attend at least a couple of them in the next twelve months.

2. Set up regular phone calls and visits to the regional sales manager; invite him to come on a couple of calls with you.

3. Jot down three or four ways in which you can save money—even if it's just a few bucks. In bad times, every dollar assumes a great importance in your budget.

Chapter 18

Managers: Learn Your Roles

The thing that continues to surprise—nay shock—me is that most sales managers have absolutely no management training. As I noted a couple of chapters ago, most tend to be former (usually successful) sales reps who were promoted without a lot of thought given about their management skills.

The problem—as many of us know—is that not everyone is cut out to be a manager. And managing a sales force is particularly difficult because we sales folks are generally independent-minded souls who often bristle at being told what to do. And managers tend to want to do things the way they did, forgetting that different reps have different styles.

Yet most of the executives who hire me to instruct their sales staffs never thought about using me to teach their managers how to manage. So let me talk (or actually write) now about what I tell managers in my course, with the understanding that everything I'm about to say increases by a factor of ten when you can find the economy in a Dumpster.

CASE IN POINT

First, the reality is that managers don't always have a direct impact on sales. I will cite the experience of sales manager Jason, who took my course a couple of years after he was appointed to the job. He worked for a large multinational company, and before he got the sales job he was an advertising manager. He and a colleague, a marketing manager, both vied for a director of marketing post, and the other guy got it. But the company didn't want to lose Jason. He'd been an adept and successful manager—and there was this opening as director of domestic sales.

The company offered the post to Jason for the wrong reasons, and he accepted it for the wrong reasons. While he was a good manager, he had never been in sales and knew nothing about sales. And had the company not been intent on keeping him, he never, ever would have been considered for this post.

Jason, on the other hand, was hurt that he didn't get the job he wanted, but the promotion offered a salve to his wounded ego—and a hefty boost in salary. Also, if he didn't take the promotion, he might have to start looking for work elsewhere.

Jason told me all this a couple of years after the fact, adding that from the moment he started he felt he was in over his head. Even his background in advertising and marketing was of little assistance. So, to compensate for his lack of knowledge, he came on like gangbusters, ordering early morning individual and group meetings as well as after-hours and weekend conferences. He was very strict about call reports and other often meaningless tasks.

The irony is that sales in his group continued to rise. The economy was great, and his people weren't going to cut off their noses to spite their faces. They went out and sold, notwithstanding Jason's interference. ✦

Why do people like Jason come and take my course? Because they know they're doing something wrong. In the example above, Jason lost a couple of his best sales reps. And though they didn't say it directly to his face, word came back that they left because of his meddling. That hurt Jason more than being passed over earlier. He'd prided himself on what he thought were his excellent management skills. And it got him to thinking. If sales were up 9 percent a year with him being a crummy manager, how much more would they have risen if he knew what he was doing? Which is what brought him to me.

The Sergeants of Sales

Here's what I tell managers like Jason:

Managers and directors are the NCOs of sales, the sergeants who actually make everything work. You are the people who rally the troops, and you are the bulwark between them and upper management. Especially upper management that's taken leave of its senses (as upper managements sometimes have a tendency to do).

For example, I know of several companies where quotas for the following year come down from on high the way Moses received the Ten Commandments. They—the quotas, not the commandments—

are often not realistic. They don't take into account the economic conditions generally or in your industry specifically. The only thing the senior managers are worried about is the short term—revenue, profits, stock prices.

There are a couple of things you as a manager can do. The first is to go to your bosses and attempt to argue logically that setting forth unattainable goals is counterproductive. You can tell senior executives that it will hurt morale, that it may cause some of your best salespeople to leave, and that a happy sales force is a productive sales force.

Or you can just beat your head against the wall, because it feels so good when you stop. So what to do?

> *Be honest*
> *with your staff.*

First of all, be honest with your staff. Realistically, it's the only choice you have. You can tell them you tried. You can tell them it's going to be a tough year. But most important, you have to tell them that you're all in this together. If you were not a true leader before, you have to explain that past is past, and that the entire group will work through this hopefully temporary crisis together. And you have to mean it.

You need to run interference. You have to stand between your staff and further management misguidedness. Those same senior management people who raised quotas are probably not through; they'll want blood from your sales stones. So there will probably be further cuts in the kinds of expenses you really need to do your job, especially in difficult times. You'll be asked to reduce travel and trade-show participation and generally take on a bunker mentality. You have to protect your people. You may not be able to salvage all the budget cuts, but you might find ways to save money in areas that are not as critical as travel and entertainment.

What can you do? Remember, it's all about attitude. And you have to set the example. Become a cheerleader. The reality is that things are probably going to get worse before they get better. Not only do your people have higher quotas, but also sales are likely to be down, cutting further into whatever commissions the reps are likely to earn. So a large part of your job is putting out a positive spin, building team spirit, doing what you can to build morale.

At the same time, remind yourself that you don't know it all. Communications is a two-way street. Ask your people for ideas. They may come up with ways to cut expenses and/or increase sales. If nothing else, they will appreciate being asked.

Become

a cheerleader.

You'll have to be especially careful about who you hire. Good enough will no longer be good enough. In a tough job market, your supervisors will expect the extraordinary from you and the people you bring aboard. In fact, management will watch every request you make and push back, asking you to make do with less.

You'll be responsible for training. No one hates saying this more than I do, but training of any kind is among the first things eliminated in tough times. Who does that leave? You—even if you don't feel qualified. That excuse won't work, because sales training won't be available the way it is in good times. It is, to me, counterintuitive, because logic would dictate that when times are bad, sales reps need to know how to work at peak efficiency. But it is what it is.

Ideally, you'll be spending more time with your reps—both independent and staff. But when things go kerblooey, nothing is ever ideal. In the real world, instead of spending windshield time with your reps, you may have to take responsibility for accounts of your own. When one of his people left, a sales manager I know was told he couldn't hire a replacement. Rather, he had to split the accounts evenly among existing staff—including himself. That meant he had to take ownership of a dozen clients, leaving him even less time to mentor and do the real work of a manager.

Finally, remember that your responsibility will increase—but your authority won't. The bosses may ask you to have bottom-line profit and loss responsibility—without the authority.

If you weren't depressed before you read this, I'm betting you almost certainly are depressed now. But what I've said to your reps in earlier chapters obviously applies to you, too. For one thing, this too shall pass. It may take a while, but the economy will pick up.

Also, you have to remain positive. Even if they don't like you, your reps take their cues from you. If you're a downer, it's an excuse for them to be down, too; it legitimizes their negativity.

Finally, this really is an opportunity to soar. Things are so bad, what have you got to lose by introducing innovative programs you've been thinking about for a while? If you do it when things are going well and you derail things, well it's pretty obvious who's to blame. On the other hand, when times are bad, there really isn't anything to derail. No problem.

Take Action

1. Think of some inexpensive morale-building activities for your staff. Maybe it's just taking them out for a round of drinks. Maybe it's going somewhere or doing something together. But put the team first.

2. When you get ready to meet with members of your staff, check your energy level. If you're down, you'll bring them down. Instead, infuse them with a new sense of purpose.

3. Don't bad-mouth the company or management to your staff. Rather, look realistically at the challenges before you and brainstorm ideas to meet them.

Chapter 19

Go After the Elephant

Years ago, when I first started my business, I did it with one big account on my books. I could have lived quite comfortably off the proceeds of that account. And while I went through the motions of getting additional business, I did so halfheartedly. There was no sense of urgency. I had a contract, after all.

Do any of you have any doubts where I'm going with this? Of course not, I'm sure. The company was bought out by an even larger one. New management was brought in. And the concept of training was devalued.

When the new human resources vice president called to say he was canceling my contract, what could I do? It wasn't like I could legally challenge the behemoth he represented. And even if I could have afforded to mount a legal fight, I probably wouldn't have. Think about it. Would you hire a trainer who sued his biggest (former) client.

My only alternative was to run to my accountant and tell him I was going out of business. He told me something I really already knew. If I had more business I wouldn't have to be afraid of losing one account—even one this large.

That's not to say you shouldn't go after the big piece of business. In fact, I've never met a sales rep who doesn't have a fantasy about winning the selling lottery—that is, landing that one big account, the whale, the elephant, that will pay for the McMansion, the vacation home on the Cape, and the Porsche (or, for my more conservative sales brethren, a Bentley).

It's a great dream, and one that you potentially can make a reality. But it is hard to do in the best of times and incrementally more difficult when times are bad. First, as a matter of course let me talk about things to keep in mind approaching an elephant when the economy is, in the words of Mazda, "zoom-zoom."

Keeping Focused

The most important thing is that you can't expect anything approaching a quick sale. The larger the company, the larger the order, the greater the bureaucracy, the more levels you have to go through.

The greatest danger in going after an elephant is that you lose focus. The idea of landing a big account becomes so all-consuming that you spend less time in cultivating new smaller accounts and pay less attention to the ones you already have in your book. Then, if the elephant falls through, you're out of luck. It's exactly what happened to me.

Don't let your grandiose dreams interfere with reality. The chances are if you do get some business from the elephant, it will be smaller than you expect. Don't even think about acting disappointed. Getting your foot in the door is a major victory.

I've never been able to come up with an easy formula defining how much time a sales rep should spend pursuing a dream. Obviously if you work at Boeing selling Dreamliners, pretty much all your time is spent dealing with elephants. But if you sell widgets, you probably don't want to forget Dave the Plumber and friends while you go after International Plumbing Supply Manufacturing Corporation. It's a balancing act each of you will have to figure out for yourselves.

Just remember that the tightrope will be farther from the ground when the economy tanks. Your perch is much more precarious, and it's more important than ever that you leave yourself a safety net.

Sales Tactic

Go after smaller companies. They are more agile. Decisions come quicker. And while each order will be smaller, you can sign up many, many more in the time you attempt to sign the elephant

If you still decide to go after the elephant, here's what you should know: In bad times, the people at larger companies are more reluctant than normal to make changes. This is a function of a number of factors. For one, there are the endless layers of bureaucracy. For another, there's self-preservation. No one wants to be the person who rocks the boat. Everyone burrows deeper into their respective foxholes, knowing that only the people who stick their necks out get hit.

Because of this siege mentality, you'll find that the larger the company (particularly in bad times), the less interest there is in something innovative. You can't turn a battleship on a dime. But you can sell something new to a smaller company. Entrepreneurial-type firms thrive on innovation.

Smaller companies are quicker off the block when it comes to making decisions. In bad times, even landing a small account can improve your morale. If you decide you have to, really need to, absolutely must go for the elephant, keep some perspective. Allow time for these morale-building smaller accounts.

In bad times, even landing a small
account can improve your morale.

Prioritize. Start off your elephant-hunting safari by going after elephants you've previously—but unsuccessfully—tried to capture. There are several advantages to this, including you likely know the players, you know the company, you know the way everything operates. Presumably, you also know what went wrong last time. Come in with a new approach. You've got nothing to lose.

If you don't have a contact in the company, don't waste your time. Remember the bigger the company, the more likely that its executives will be buried in their foxholes avoiding the next round of layoffs. They won't have the time or inclination to see someone they don't even know. The answer: networking. More than ever, now is the time to check your Rolodex. If there are only six degrees of separation between you and Kevin Bacon, there will probably be less than that between you and the purchasing manager at Global International Elephants, Inc.

"Mr. Jones, Charlie Watts of Rolling Stones, Inc., gave me your name. He thinks you'd be interested in my widgets."

If you've done the networking right, the prospect will see you out of loyalty to Charlie Watts. But that doesn't mean you're going to make much sales progress there, at least right away. In the beginning, at least, it's primarily about building a relationship. You're not going to become the prospect's friend. She probably has enough friends already, and a lunch isn't going to get you any business.

Don't even attempt to sell. If you get your foot in the door, there's no reason you can't say that this meeting is just about getting to know each other. You appreciate that she took time to see you. Building a relationship is key and can accomplish three important goals.

First, the prospect, let's call her Donna, will almost certainly report back to the person who got the two of you together; let's call her Barbara. If Donna tells Barbara, "I met with Frank (that's you) and he's a really nice guy," it will reaffirm Barbara's faith in you and make her more confident to recommend you to others.

Second, when Donna reports to Barbara she will likely also say, "I don't have anything right now for Frank, but I'll certainly keep him in mind." And she probably will, whether the company decides to revisit your product over the short term or months from now when the economy is good—or at least better.

Third, elephants are big and run around in huge herds. Donna may not need you, but she may know another member of the herd who does.

In bad times, I think you build a relationship with the elephant first and only then do you begin the genuine sales process. Only then will the world's Donnas be open to discussing it.

Take Action

1. For every big company on your list of prospects, come up with two or three smaller companies that you can add to the list.

2. List some big accounts you've gone after (unsuccessfully) in the past. Rethink your approach to them. Now that times are tough, what can you offer them? Can your product or service solve a problem for them?

Chapter 20

Prospecting (Part One)

I'm going to repeat a point I made in the previous chapter. You need to stay on top of existing business. In the example I gave, I didn't, and I unexpectedly lost a longtime account. Had I been more aware of what was going on there, I might have been able to save the business. Or at least I might have concentrated more on getting new business.

This can be interpreted in a couple of ways. Obviously, you might think that you caught me in a do-what-I-say-not-what-I-do moment. And you'd be correct. But I prefer to think of it as a valuable illustration of how even sales professionals hate to make cold calls. And, equally to the point, when times are good, we tend to slack off doing things we don't want to do—that is, prospecting. But that ultimately and inevitably leads to bad times. Because in the same way that it happened to me, some accounts are going to fall by the wayside.

Your contacts will be promoted, transferred, fired, or will quit or retire—and their replacements just don't see the light.

Your client companies will be shuttered, merge with other companies, or close production lines—leaving you out in the cold.

You'll be stuck up a high-mortgage creek without a commission paddle. Why? Because you didn't cold call. You didn't keep adding a steady stream of new clients.

Because getting and retaining business becomes so very much more difficult in these times, it is more important than ever that you stick to the proven basics. It is urgent that you resist the temptation—as I was unable to—to slough off.

> *It is more important than ever*
> *that you stick to the proven basics.*

It will be difficult. We've spoken about ratios. In the past, to create an example, you may have needed to make twenty calls to get through to five people. And of those five people you got one appointment. And you managed a sale every three appointments. Extrapolating backward, *you made one sale every sixty calls.* That's a lot of effort. Worse, that's a lot of nos. A lot of phone calls that aren't returned. A lot of frustration, perhaps even anger.

And that's when times are good!

In times like this, where everyone is cutting back, the frustration is magnified. Instead of sixty calls to land a sale, it may take ninety or more. It's no wonder that in tough times people get depressed. It's no wonder that they wind up going through the motions without thinking.

As I write this, I periodically look out the window of a vacation home I have in Pennsylvania. I watch a woman with a leaf blower blowing leaves off her property. And as soon as she moves elsewhere, the leaves blow back. So she returns and does it all over again, and eventually her entire front lawn is clean—for about five minutes on this windy day.

And that—blowing leaves on a windy fall day—to me is a perfect illustration of what I mean when I talk about the difficulty of selling in a difficult environment. On any other day, blowing leaves works. But it won't work today. So you have to approach things a little differently. Instead of blowing them randomly, get the leaves into a pile and bag them. Or get them in a pile, rake them onto a tarp and drag them far into the woods where they won't blow back even in a hurricane.

My neighbor was doing the right thing. By that I mean she was sticking with the basics, that is, she needed to get her lawn clear of leaves. But she was doing it the same way she did it every year without regard to the conditions. That's silly. It's futile. What's the point? There is always a better way to get a job done. And so it is with sales.

Here are some rules that you may find helpful:

1. *Not making cold calls will leave you dead in the water.* It may take three months. It may take six months. But at some point the combination of less business from established clients and no new business will leave you in your own version of a Bermuda Triangle. So the first and most important rule is that you actually have to pick up the phone and call. That sounds so ridiculous—but only to people who aren't in sales and don't know how tough it is. It's difficult for actors to go on auditions; however that's the only way they're going to get work. So no mater how many times they get turned down, if they're serious about acting, they keep auditioning. Consider cold calls your audition for success.

2. *You will have to do much more preparation than you did previously.* Remember, you are not the only one who is likely to be depressed. The prospect you're trying to contact may also be wondering about the future of his job or his company. You will need to work that much harder to get him or her on the phone, and if you're successful there, you'll need to be impressive pretty quickly. Demonstrating knowledge and preparation are good ways to do that.

3. *Be positive!* There is enough depression going around. I know I've said this before, but it merits repetition. A positive attitude will set you apart. People tend to respond in kind. If you're up, they're likely to become positive—raising the level of the conversation and your odds of getting an appointment.

4. *On the subject of respond in kind: People respond not only in terms of the tone of the conversation, but directly to the questions being asked.* Keep your goals in mind and your conversation focused. Don't introduce extraneous topics that are likely to take you both off on tangents.

5. *You're only fooling yourself.* If you set a goal to make twenty cold calls every day, calling someone for the fourth time and leaving your fourth voice mail doesn't count—except as wasting your time.

Make the calls significant!

6. *More than ever, it's important to be prepared for objections.* People will find all kinds of excuses to end the conversation. You, on the other hand, have to be prepared to keep it going. Because as long as you're talking you still have a shot at convincing the prospect of the wisdom of using your product or service.

In the next chapter, I'm going to discuss some of my cold calling techniques.

Take Action

1. Set a quota of cold calls per day. And stick to it, no matter what! Set aside a specific time every day for cold calling.

2. Review how you make cold calls and to whom. Remember that things are different now; you're in a downturn and companies are cutting back on spending. Adjust your script accordingly.

3. Before you pick up the phone to make that first call, get your energy level up. Take a walk, drink another cup of coffee, do jumping jacks. Whatever it takes. Because it's your attitude that will make the sale.

Chapter 21

Prospecting (Part Two)

I have OCD-O. That is, I suffer from what might be considered obsessive compulsive disorder—occasionally. As I noted in the last chapter, in times of plenty, I have been known to skip out in cold calling. But it always catches up on me. And then I jump back in compulsively. Because I need to be obsessive and force myself to do things a certain way for a long period of time—at least until it becomes a habit.

What do I mean? Consider this:

Cold calling starts a day earlier. Before I leave the office, no matter how bad a day I've had, I sit down and go over my calendar for the next day. If I'm going to lecture or speak somewhere, I gather everything I need. If I have an outside sales appointment I gather everything I need. And if I'm going to be in the office, I gather everything I need. In the office in the morning I make cold calls. I organize five things to prepare:

- The name of the company
- The name of the person I want to contact
- His or her (preferably direct) phone number
- The research I've done on his firm
- The approach I'm going to take when I get him on the phone

Make the most
obvious calls first.

This achieves several goals for me. The most obvious is it forces me to actually come in and make calls. After putting in that effort, I'm certainly not going to let the calls slide. Second, it really prepares me. I'll be thinking about it off and on the whole night. A number of my best sales pitches come to me while I am asleep. Finally, it forces me to hone my list. As I review it the night before, I eliminate desperation calls—the kind you make only when you've tried absolutely everything else first.

I make the most obvious calls first. For example, I keep a tickler list of companies I've done business with before. After I finish a training program, I make a note to contact them again in three years, when turnover of sales reps might justify a repeat visit. Also high on the list are people who've (happily) bought my services before and moved on to new positions—either within the company or elsewhere.

I stay in touch with former clients on a regular basis, anyway. I don't make sales pitches. But I ask how things are going and exchange scuttlebutt. Even if the person I'm calling doesn't need my services, she may know someone who does.

Sales Tactic

I keep my ear to the ground. Whatever industry you're in usually has a grapevine. You hear about people you know and have dealt with getting new jobs. The first thing I do when I open a trade magazine is turn to the "People" section to see who is where. This is particularly important in bad times when there is so much turnover. People are losing jobs. Sometimes they're not replaced, but often they are. That means if there's a switcheroo at an existing client, you have to rush in to protect your turf.

If it takes place at a nonclient, perhaps at a company where you've had little success before, it might represent an opportunity.

Also high on my priority list are companies that do the same kinds of things as some of the companies where I've conducted successful programs. I already have expertise in that industry, a track record I can point to, and I can hit the ground running.

I think these examples all are reasonably logical. But what happens when I run out of companies where I have obvious connections? Next I go to large companies, which are more likely to have training programs. I belong to several training associations, and I use membership directories to give me the names of people I need to contact. (This also highlights the importance of networking, which I talked about earlier.)

At the bottom of my list are large companies where I don't know the name of the appropriate person to call or small firms where I have a shot but am unlikely to pick up a big and profitable piece of business.

Clearly, your priority list will be different from mine. But it is urgent that you have one and that your list is logical.

You Have to Get Someone on the Phone

As far as I'm concerned, the toughest part of the prospecting process is getting someone on the phone. There is a lot of interference between you and a potential client, including receptionists, secretaries, personal assistants, and voice mail. I used to hate voice mail, but I've come to favor it over all the other obstacles in my way. Human interference makes mistakes. They get messages wrong, misspell names, and don't always deliver the little pink "While You Were Out" sheets.

With voice mail on the other hand, the prospect not only gets to hear your message directly, but with your inflection and emphasis. I make notes on all my calls, and if I have a highly ranked prospect who hasn't returned one or two messages left with a secretary, I call him or her back before business hours. That way I improve my odds of getting the prospect before his various assistants can intercept my call or—at the very least—get his voice mail.

CASE IN POINT

Typically I leave a message that involves some kind of real or imagined networking, a message they can relate to. If there's someone's name I can use, I use it. "Brian Johnson suggested I call about a program I have he thought might be of interest."

Otherwise I try to network corporately. That is, I'll say something like: "I just finished a sales training program for XYZ Corporation (a company similar to the one I'm calling). It's something I'd like to discuss with you, because the results may surprise you." ✦

Don't be obsequious. I never start a conversation by apologizing for taking up their time or telling them I know how busy they must be. I'm here to help their companies do whatever they do better than they did in the past and make more money. It's their job to listen to me. I don't come across as arrogant, but being servile sends the wrong kind of message about the direction our (potential) relationship should take.

> *I never start a conversation by apologizing for taking up their time.*

Instead, be targeted. I noted earlier in this chapter that when I prepare for cold calling the night before, among the things I get ready is the pitch I'm going to use. There are a couple of key points here:

The first is that I don't use a one-size-fits-all canned pitch. Once

I get a prospect on the phone, I tailor what I'm going to say for every call. Second, I don't have a prepared speech. That inevitably comes off sounding like I'm a telemarketer. Instead, I have an outline of the points I want to make and fit them into the flow of the conversation.

It's important to know every objection. As a function of my preparation (and experience) I know just about any objection a prospect is likely to raise. And I have a response prepared. "Sorry, Steve, but we don't train our sales reps." "Then how do you prepare new hires to go out into the field?"

Historically, people communicate by telling stories. Every objection is based on a story, and if you can get a prospect to tell you his or her story, you are therefore communicating. And communicating is the first step to making a sale. As long as you communicate, you'll be able to find out what the issues are—and perhaps even how to overcome any obstacles. Also, as long as you are communicating, you have a chance to move on to the next step—an initial meeting.

Take Action

1. Go over your list of companies to cold call. Then go over it again. Remember, it's all about communication.

2. For each call, include in your notes the people you had to go through in order to get to the prospect. Wherever possible, get the prospect's direct number before you get off the phone.

3. Subscribe to three or four industry magazines or websites, and read them regularly.

Chapter 22

Go to the Government

The key to success in bad economic times is to keep the pipeline full. That means attracting a steady stream of new customers. That, of course, is difficult under the best of circumstances, and virtually impossible when the economy is tanking.

That, anyway, is conventional thinking. But conventional thinking isn't going to get any of us anywhere in bad times. One obvious place where you may not have looked before is in the area of the government. Let's face it. Who else still has money—much of it yours? Even in the worst of times, when the government is handing out money as fast as it can print it, your federal, state, and local officials still have to buy paper clips and paper and computers and ink and so on and so on and so on.

Clearly there are opportunities there for you, depending upon what you sell and whether your company is prepared to sell to the government. Let's start with the difficult part first. It is not easy. While all levels of government have simplified the process of applying for and getting government business, it can still be cumbersome. And breaking in to government sales can be frustrating. A lot of it depends on what you sell and the size of your company.

But selling to the government directly is only one of the benefits of dealing with the various levels of government. Doing so also opens you to the possibility of finding contractors already entrenched in government sales that you can subcontract with.

> *The key to success in bad economic times*
> *is to keep the pipeline full.*

For example, one of my clients manufactures security film that is put on glass windows. This film can do everything from helping to regulate temperature to providing blast protection. They operate with a kind of franchise system, and we're encouraging these regional reps to get in touch with not only construction contractors working on major government projects, but also building management companies that run buildings with federal offices.

First, you need to be aware of several websites:

- *www.fedbizopps.gov*
- *www.ccr.gov*
- *www.governmentbids.com*
- *www.gsa.gov*

Each of these important websites is relatively easy to navigate and can provide important tools for you. But nothing is simple.

If you work for a large company, the chances are that someone somewhere above your pay grade has already figured out that the government can be a good customer. If that's the case, there probably already is a national account manager charged with working to get federal business.

What role can you play? There isn't one simple answer to that question. But depending upon your company, what it sells, how its sales unit—that is, you—is set up (locally, regionally or nationally), there still can be a role for you.

Find Out Your Government Status

Frankly, this is something your manager, your director, and your regional vice president might not have thought of yet. There's no downside to this. If there is someone handling government sales, you still come off as someone thinking outside the box, someone who hasn't succumbed to the negative vibes prevalent throughout the business world. If there's no one handling government sales, it may be an opening for you to move into that area.

If There is Someone in the Slot, Work with Him or Her

One person can't do it all. Chances are if your company has a government rep, that person—let's call her Barbara just to make my life easier—is based near the nation's capital. Call her. See if there's anything you can do to help from wherever your outpost is. Ask for advice on picking up regional business. Check that it's okay to register for opportunities with the state governments in your area and with counties and municipalities as well.

Small Companies Do Even Better

Governments at all levels have set-asides for small businesses that meet certain criteria. If you are independently owned, not the dominant company in your field, and fall within financial guidelines that vary from industry to industry, you may qualify. A good place to start is at the Small Business Administration website, *www.sba.gov.* It will guide you through the labyrinth and help you find your North American Industry Classification System (NAICS) numbers and register in Central Contractor Registration.

Ask!

Surprisingly—and contrary to the image perpetuated by Department of Motor Vehicle employees—government employees in the contracting area are generally very helpful. There are even dedicated 800 numbers to help you and your company get registered. Every bid put out has a contract officer to whom you can direct questions.

All Sales Are Local

Remember what I said early on about all sales being local? Well that applies to government sales as well. Especially if you are a small company with only regional capabilities, be sure to register at the state, county, and municipal level.

There's More Than Contracting Work Available

Depending upon what you sell, there are also opportunities for subcontracting work. Many of these websites post who won the contracts. Check those lists because there may be subcontracting opportunities with companies you hadn't thought of before.

It doesn't happen all the time, but it does happen: you go prospecting and you strike gold.

Take Action

1. Check out directories of government offices and departments. Check off those for which your product or service might provide a solution to a problem.

2. Read the website of the Small Business Administration on a regular basis.

3. Find out who in your sales force has dealt with government contracts before. Take that person out to lunch and pick his brain. He's probably got lots of good tips on how to circumnavigate the bureaucracy.

Chapter 23

The Power of Twelve

The Power of Twelve is a phrase I coined to describe a system that serves a couple of significant purposes. Those of you who've read my previous books or attended one of my seminars are no doubt familiar with the expression. I will explain it for those of you who are not. And then I will go on to spell out why it is so important in bad times.

At its simplest, the Power of Twelve provides information that will increase your odds of closing a sale. But it is also a way to further entrench yourself in a company and find additional business opportunities.

> *The Power of Twelve*
> *provides information that will*
> *increase your odds of closing a sale.*

Let me illustrate how it works. I've had a first or second meeting with a prospect, and it's gone well. Normally at this stage of a relationship, most sales reps would begin to circle in for the kill. I advise against it, for a lot of reasons. First of all, you probably don't have enough information. Your prospect, for the sake of argument, is the purchasing manager. He may be working off of and providing you with dry statistics from some engineer's spec sheet. But that never gives you the nuances of the product.

And even if you are working with someone familiar with the fundamentals of what you are trying to sell, it is still only one point of view. More than likely, there are other forces at play. Someone may be happy with the product your potential customer is using but unhappy with customer service. Another element may be that the customer service is so good because the product stinks and your competitor improved customer service just to soothe ruffled feathers. But unless you ask, you'll never know.

What I usually say to the prospect is something like this:

"I'd like to make a proposal, but I really want it to be on target. So what I'd like to do is visit with some of your salespeople, perhaps go out on a call with a couple of them, so I can make a more intelligent proposal."

> *The deeper you penetrate*
> *into a company,*
> *the greater the likelihood*
> *you'll wind up*
> *with a signed contract.*

Depending upon what you sell, you may want to visit with workers on the assembly line or the vice president of manufacturing or, if it's a small company, the president him or herself. Twelve is the number I picked because I've found that visiting with more than a dozen people in a firm tends to be counterproductive. You wind up hearing the same things over and over again. But when you sell to a small company, there may not be a dozen people to see. You have to use your own judgment. But as a rule, twelve works well.

Just remember, the deeper you penetrate into a company, the greater the likelihood you'll wind up with a signed contract.

Some points here.

Not everyone will give you free rein. But you have nothing to lose by asking. It's up to you to make a strong case for why you should be permitted into the inner sanctum. In some ways this may be easier in hard times than it is when times are good. The chances are greater that up and down the corporate ladder, executives are looking for ways to cut expenses and increase revenues. I tell prospects something like this:

"I have a proven record of coming into a company and increasing sales. But I don't have a one-size-fits-all training program. Your sales problems are probably different from XYZ Corporation, where sales grew 15 percent after I finished my program there. I can probably run a boilerplate program, but frankly I believe that will be setting up both of us for failure. I'd rather take the extra time, spend it with your sales reps, speak to your executives. I'd even like to talk to your customers. The more information I have, the better I'll be able to tailor a meaningful program just for you."

You can do a variation on this theme. You may need to see how your product is installed on the prospect's assembly line to see if you can figure out a less expensive way to do that or to see if there's a way you can cut costs.

The point is that you improve your chances of getting an okay through the Power of Twelve if you can show specifically how your product will help improve the prospect's bottom line.

Don't limit yourself by title. The temptation is to concentrate the Power of Twelve on corporate executives, and certainly that's necessary for reasons I'll go into a little later. But the higher up the corporate ladder you go, the farther away you are from the end user. The key to your sale may be some little tidbit you pick up in the factory.

CASE IN POINT

A sales rep I trained once told me he followed my advice. He went into a factory, spoke to a few of the blue collar workers there who told him they were unhappy with the widgets the company was currently using. They were difficult to install and forced them to stop the assembly line on a regular basis to readjust components. Though my former student's widgets were more expensive, he was able to make the case that they'd be less expensive in the long run because they were of better quality and easier to use. He got the sale. ✦

One of my rules is, always ask for more. Usually, your prospect will give you the names of two or three people or, if you're lucky, actually set up meetings with them. That's generally not sufficient. So I always ask each Power of Twelve interview a simple question: "Is there anyone you think I should speak to?" And you can build from there.

> *One of my rules is,*
> *always ask for more.*

Another rule—and this is a really important one—is always be grateful. Obviously, conclude each interview by thanking the person you've spoken to for his or her time. But especially, when applicable (and even sometimes when it isn't), I also tell them the information they've given me has provided me with important insight into the way their product/service is or can be used, and I plan to incorporate that into my presentation.

Why? The main benefit of the Power of Twelve is that it can provide you with the information resources you need. But there are additional advantages, as well. For one, it provides an opportunity to win allies in the company. Let's say you speak to the vice president of manufacturing and, based upon your conversation, are able to address his concerns; he will probably become an ally of yours. If someone provides you with a revelatory kernel of info, he or she becomes vested in you.

Another important point, especially in larger corporations: you may wind up talking to someone who can provide you access to possible customers in other divisions of the same company or sister companies under the same corporate umbrella.

The Power of Twelve in Bad Times

But much of this information is true no matter what the state of the economy. What makes it so important now? There are several reasons.

You Need the Business

The Power of Twelve is an important tool when times are good. But it is especially important now. When times are good, you can get away with murder and still clinch a sale. Maybe you don't cold call every day. Perhaps you decide the Power of Twelve is unnecessary. But when every sale counts, it is urgent that you walk the line, you dot every i and cross every t. When the economy is in the tank, you need to seize every opportunity available to you, and the Power of Twelve may be among your greatest shots at clinching the sale.

You Need to Be on Top of all the Changes

The world is turning topsy-turvy. Everything that you held to be true once upon a time may prove a fairy tale. The American automobile industry will be designing different cars that require lighter but structurally sounder widgets. It will be more careful in choosing suppliers. It will ask more of them. And unless you are entrenched in a company, unless you have access to key people, you may not discover changes relevant to your potential success.

New Industries Will Be Born

I recently read an article about a new "industry" that's emerged: medical tourism. That is, companies are sponsoring tours for people going to countries where medical procedures are cheaper than in the United States. Something just like this might emerge in the industries you serve. Before the downturn, I limited use of the Power of Twelve to reps calling on potential new clients. But the way the economy is changing, I think it's important also to regularly touch base with Powers of Twelve in accounts you already have. This is especially true if people really like what you've done. Now more than ever it's important to network with people who will sing your praises and recommend you to people who might become customers as well as keep you appraised of changes at their company.

Finally, do not assume just because you've spoken to a dozen people that you've got it all down correctly. After I finish my Power of Twelve but well before I even think about preparing a presentation, I go back to my contact to be "righted." That is, I check out the things I've learned and my conclusions to discover if I'm on the correct path. It's only then that I start thinking about what and when I'm going to present.

Take Action

1. Talk to as many people at the target company as possible. And don't just talk—listen. That's the most important part of the Power of Twelve.

2. Go back over your steady accounts and review how much information you have about them. If you need more, use the Power of Twelve and start asking questions.

3. Don't just ask questions about the company. Ask about the industry and issues beyond the industry. You'll get some insights that may lead you to an entirely new area for prospecting.

Chapter 24

Give Killer Presentations

As any experienced salesperson knows, by the time you get to the presentation stage during a normal sales process, the odds are pretty good that you've clinched a sale—or at least you have a pretty good idea of what the outcome will be. Nothing in life is guaranteed, but if you've followed all the steps, that is, done your research and spoken to enough people, you can tell from the reaction you've received what your reception will be when it comes to a presentation.

But when times are not so good, nothing is assured. And as it is with every other step in the sales process, you will have to be at the top of your game. What does that mean?

Recognize that it's the message, not the medium. If you want to make a sale, fancy presentations alone aren't going to cut it any longer. There has to be a meaningful advantage to using your product and service rather than that of your competitors. If you've done the Power of Twelve properly, you will have found out what your prospect's pain is. Is it just price? Is it service? Is it quality? Those are the issues you should be addressing—not how to doll up your PowerPoint.

Before the presentation, get a copy of the guest list. It's important to know not only how many people will attend your presentation, but also who they are. If they are people you've already spoken to, you have a good idea of what their concerns are and where they stand vis-à-vis your product or service. You can address their worries and, as a result, be reasonably certain of their support. But if there are people you don't know, see if you can get in touch with them in advance. Explain that you've already spoken to many of the people on the committee and you want to bring them up to date on what you've learned. Ask: "Are these issues of concern to you, as well?" It is helpful to know who is on your team and who isn't.

> *It's the message,*
> *not the medium.*

Do not memorize your presentation. If you do that, you risk coming off sounding like a telemarketer. Also, you will probably be flummoxed if someone interrupts you to ask a question. Make an outline of the points you want to cover on index cards you can refer to if you get lost.

While it may be tempting to throw in a lot of fancy computer slides, my advice is to use your computer, but don't let it use you. Because computers have become increasingly powerful, software manufacturers have been able to add all kinds of bells and whistles to their products. Clearly, what you can do with PowerPoint today is much more sophisticated than what you could do with it as recently as a decade ago. But that's usually if you follow some preformatted sample. I don't know a lot of salespeople who can create a sophisticated presentation from scratch—that is without the help of Microsoft's engineers. There's nothing wrong with that. It's perfectly okay to follow a format—so long as you don't allow it to control you. Remember, fancy presentations don't sell. Quality ideas do.

> *Keep it simple.*

Here's another basic rule: *KISS*. That's right. Keep it simple, uh, silly. You don't need fancy art work or graphics. A good presentation begins when you state the key points you want to make. For example, "I'm going to save you money on your widgets and provide better service and quality." You follow that by explaining how you will do it and asking for questions. Occasionally you may be able to get approval for a deal right then, but more likely you'll have to check in again. Don't wait too long. Call your contact within two or three days, while your presentation is still fresh in his or her mind.

Don't do something stupid, silly, part one. Go over your slides with a fine-tooth comb. Better still, have your manager or a colleague do so. How embarrassing would it be for you to have some ridiculous spelling mistake on a screen or to use the wrong word—say, *your*, when you mean *you're*. I've seen it happen. In fact, if it is at all possible, go over the entire presentation. There may be gaps in logic that you don't see because you are too close to the forest.

Don't do something stupid, silly, part two. Obviously, you cannot make rude racial, ethnic, or sexual comments under any circumstances. I said "obviously," but I've seen it happen. A man making a presentation to a group of men made a crude comment about a woman competitor. I think he meant it as a joke. But whether he realized it or not, that joke immediately eliminated him from the competition. No one wants to do business with a crude person. Your crudeness reflects on your product or service, and it will reflect on anyone who does business with you.

Don't do something stupid, silly, part three. Avoid humor. The problem is that what you believe is funny may not be funny to your audience. There is no worse feeling than standing in front of a group having told a story or anecdote you were convinced would kill, and hearing deathly silence. At best, you'll be embarrassed. In the worst case, you'll be thrown so far off your game that you'll flub the rest of your presentation.

On the day of the presentation arrive early and check out the room. Be sure your presentation will be visible from every corner. If not, see if you can rearrange the furniture or the screens so everyone can see your work. Bring extension cords and extra batteries for your laptop.

The most important key to giving a killer presentation is you've got to trust in yourself. If you've done all the work you were supposed to, if your proposal matches the prospect company's needs, you have nothing to worry about. There is no sense worrying about things you can't control—internal politics, for example. Win, lose, or draw, you've done your job.

Take Action

1. Rehearse your presentation, preferably with an audience. Give it to a group of your coworkers and ask them to critique it.

2. Go over your PowerPoint slides before the presentation. You can't fix a mistake once it's been projected on the screen and everyone's looking at it.

3. Get your energy level up before the presentation. If you feel good about what you're saying, chances are your audience will too.

Chapter 25

Nothing Is Forever

All of the foregoing has been premised on the idea that by returning to the basics, you can overcome challenges that bad times throw at you. There's no magical solution—just a lot of hard work. But there may come a point in your sales career when you have to decide whether there are greener pastures elsewhere. That's something people who know me never thought they'd hear me say. Quite frankly, I'm surprised myself.

I've always enjoyed the challenge of the sale. For me, it was like war without the blood—just the sweat and tears. But to quote Bob Dylan, the times they are a-changin'.

So let's talk about what options you have. The first thing you have to consider is your age. I know. There's no such thing as age discrimination. In fact, every company you apply to has probably placed help-wanted ads looking for fifty-five- to sixty-year-old sales reps. I'm not suggesting that you don't have a shot at getting another position, but it won't be easy.

Another consideration is how long you've been with your present company. If you're one of the lucky few who works for a company that still has a pension plan or some other matching benefit program such as a 401(k), that will need to be factored into whatever decision you make.

For example, let's suppose you have three years in the plan and will be fully vested in just two more. Does it pay to move and possibly lose three years' worth of employer contributions? Or are you better off trying to hang in there. Let's go to the other extreme. Let's say you're in your early sixties and actually found another job. You intend to work another two or three or four years—so that for all practical purposes you won't be accruing much if any retirement benefits if you leave your present position. Do you try to hang in for a few more years?

> *There may come a point in your sales career*
> *when you have to decide whether*
> *there are greener pastures elsewhere.*

I'm not the right person to ask what you should do in any of these scenarios. You will no doubt have to consult your accountant. I mention this only to give you an idea of how complex the situation can be—particularly when there aren't a lot of jobs out there.

Like many of you, I regularly check the Internet sales job sites, and I can tell you that, recently, examining these sites has taken me a lot less time. There's less to look at, and those jobs that are listed more often than not are for lower-level, lower-salary/commission positions.

So what may be a simple decision in normal times becomes complicated and extremely important. And it becomes complicated to write about, as well, because there are so many variables. Do you want to leave because you fear that your company is about to go under? Are you concerned about your job? Has your income been cut drastically? Or do you just hate your boss?

Sometimes the decision is made for you. If you lose your job for whatever reason, you have to find another job. But what about the other times? What do you do then? Well, you have several options:

1. *Never stop looking.* The idea of corporate loyalty to employees is very nineteenth century. What that means is that you should never,

ever stop looking to see what's available in the marketplace. Even if you're happy and the economy is purring like a cat on nip, you owe it to yourself to understand what's going on in the marketplace.

2. *Stay put.* In the same way that there are situations where you have to leave, there are situations where you have to stay. For example, if there are no jobs out there, even the worst position is better than unemployment insurance. Keep in mind that at some point things will change. At some point the economy will get better. And things will return back to the way they were before. You need to ask yourself if you were happy before.

3. *Find another job.* In this economy, that's easier said than done. But the reality is finding a job is just another form of selling. The only difference is that now you're selling yourself. And who ever had a better product? The same rules apply. Network. Cold call. Find a compelling reason why you should be hired. Emphasize your product's strengths and how it—you—will help the prospect's company make more money. Close the sale.

4. *Don't leave in a huff.* You don't want to burn bridges. You never know when you'll need to cross that one again. At the very least, you may want (need) a recommendation. Also, decisions made in anger usually are impulsive . . . and wrong.

5. *Leave sales entirely.* One of the things I'm noted for is my honesty. (Though some prefer to call me blunt.) Sales is a tough gig under the best of circumstances. It's easy to burn out, more so when every sale becomes a minor war. It's understandable. What do you do? The most logical move is to something else in the industry you're in. Presumably you have contacts and know the business. There may be an opening in a marketing slot somewhere that allows you to use your knowledge and skills.

Start Your Own Business

Another possibility is becoming an entrepreneur. As a sales rep you were in a very real way running your own business, and that ability is transferable. You can buy an existing company or purchase a franchise. The latter normally is an easier transition, because you have the support of a home office. Where possible, you should try to find a business where you can use the skills you've accumulated over the years.

But remember, money is tight, and it may be hard to get financing. Nothing is easy in this economy. Still . . .

CASE IN POINT

I recently advised a friend of mine that his best bet might be to go into business for himself. He was a sales executive frustrated by politics and decided he no longer wanted the corporate life.

His response was no, not interested, because he was concerned that if things didn't work out he could lose everything he'd worked for. I told him that it was that kind of thinking that keeps people locked into unhappy situations. Sure, he could wind up losing a lot of money, and no one wants to do that. But life is too short for unhappiness. And there's never really a good time for anything—marriage, kids, or starting a business. There's always a negative. ✦

I'm not a job-hunting expert. I'm not a psychologist or an accountant. The point I'm trying to make here is that you have choices. Some may be made for you. Some are difficult. But what you do in the successful sales process you need to do in your life, and that is take control.

Take Action

1. Check the job listings in your field every week. You don't have to apply for anything, but keep looking. It never hurts.

2. If you feel as if you want to leave your job, make a list of the reasons to leave. Then make another list of the reasons to stay. Walk away from the list for a couple of days or a week and then come back and see how you feel.

3. If you're unhappy, talk to someone. Maybe it's your spouse, a coworker, someone else in the field. But don't bottle up your emotions; that's not good for you and not good for your job performance.

Chapter 26

The New Sales Model

Authors normally do not dedicate book chapters. I know I never have—in the past. But I think it highly appropriate to dedicate these next few pages to Friedrich Nietzsche.

Nietzsche is the German philosopher who most famously said: "That which does not destroy us makes us stronger."

I suspect that the reason I chose him is obvious. We're going through very difficult times now. Not everyone will make it through to better days. Some companies will go under. Some sales reps will, too. But those who survive will be stronger for the experience. I also believe that because you are sufficiently concerned about your career, you will be one of the survivors.

The experience you undergo when times are as bad as they are now (at least as this is written and supposedly for the foreseeable future) will certainly make you stronger, but will it make you wiser? Change is in the air. The question is are you going to take advantage and use what you learn now in the future?

What will happen when the economy starts to rebound? For one thing, corporate executives are not going to forget what they've been through and that will mean significant changes in the way we work.

For one thing, I believe there will be no more gatherers. Traditionally I've divided sales reps into two types: there are the hunters and the gatherers. The hunters are the aggressive sales folks who pursue game. Gatherers are order takers. I don't think there is much of a market left for gatherers.

Again, drawing on the past, I've said it's imperative for salespeople to rise above being "merely" salespeople and become trusted advisors. When times are bad and the economy's tanking, we have to have to do better than that; we have to have to become partners, at least to our biggest clients. Everyone will be doing their best to cut costs and demanding additional support from their suppliers. It may be in further cost cuts, increased promotional funds to extended terms—or any other of perhaps a dozen or more opportunities. The more you partner, the more you sell.

> *The more you partner,*
> *the more you sell.*

Sales Tactic

Above all other tactics to employ in a downturn, my advice to you is don't forget to soar. Don't you forget the lessons you've learned, either. Creativity, an approach that differentiates you (in a positive way) will lead you to success. The expression "thinking outside the box" has become something of a cliché. But if you can train yourself to dismiss tired old ideas and keep plugging away until something new and innovative hits your neurons, then you'll do quite well in the new sales model.

Thank goodness that you're not starting out in sales during a downturn. When the economy goes south, newcomers will find it much more difficult to get work that isn't based entirely on commissions. The job landscape will change too. More will be expected of you. But if you're good, if you adapt, you'll enjoy great success.

But understand that some things never change. I recently ran across a quote from Sam Wyly, a billionaire entrepreneur who started and/or expanded almost a dozen businesses. He said:

"When a customer says no, that's when the selling begins."

Take Action

1. Read this book again. Think about it. Discuss it with your coworkers.

2. Soar.

Chapter 27

Conclusion

When I first started my career as a sales consultant, I knew it all. Incomprehensibly, there were actually much older people stuck in a previous century who tried to give me advice. What were they thinking? Didn't they know who they were talking to? What was the point? Either I was already aware of what they were saying or their advice was ridiculous and only worthy of my contempt.

Let me give you an example. Early on in my career—I was probably in my early thirties—I was hired to give a pilot class by a large corporation. I worked with a woman from the human resources department who was much older than I; I'm guessing she was a dinosaur in her mid-forties. If she approved, I'd be on the receiving end of a substantial piece of business.

Let's call her Miss Smith, as a sign of respect for her ancient condition (and the fact that back then there was no such thing as Ms. Anyway, Miss Smith audited my class and evaluated my methodology and I guess me. At first she showed brilliance; she began by telling me how much she loved what I did and how helpful she thought it would be.

But then she had to ruin it all by offering a "suggestion." For some reason, Miss Smith thought it would be helpful if I interrupted what I was doing to offer a brief review of what I'd done. No fool I, I responded with "Yes, ma'am. Good idea ma'am." Of course all along

I'm thinking it might be time for her to check into a nursing home. My students weren't stupid. They could follow along quite easily.

To make a short story long, I got the contract, and when I taught at Miss Smith's company I did what she wanted. And you know what? She was actually right. What I discovered was that I was throwing so much new at the students, it was easy for many of them to get lost. Stopping to review material was helpful in that it brought everyone up to speed and made it easier to move on.

In this book, I've tried to make a few basic points, based on a lifetime of experience selling, both in good times and in bad. Here are the main things I want you to take away from our time together:

1. *The economy is cyclical.* If you started your career in an up cycle, chances are you're going to experience a downturn. Likewise, if things look very black at the moment and companies are cutting personnel and products left and right, somewhere over the horizon the sun is shining brightly on a new business world.

2. *There's no magic formula for selling in a bad economy.* At the risk of seeming redundant, let me repeat: There's no magic formula for selling in a bad economy. You can't just "sell harder" (whatever that means) or "sell more." What you can do is return to the fundamentals. Sell like the best salesperson you know how to be.

3. *Selling in an economic downturn means looking at things in a different way.* All the low-hanging fruit that was available when times were better isn't there any more. Instead, you've got increasingly frustrated salespeople struggling for an ever-shrinking piece of the pie. But if you're smart, you'll see opportunities where others see problems. You'll see that hard times free you to be more inventive, more creative, more wildly innovative about how you're selling and where you're selling.

4. *Hard times are also a chance to transform your relationship with your accounts.* It's not just about selling to them. Instead, it's about helping them find new solutions to their problems. That kind of soaring is going to bring rich rewards when the economy wobbles back toward center and business starts picking up. The accounts are going to remember who helped them during that long, dark night.

5. *Finally, as I've never ceased to say in all my books, sales is about attitude.* If you can maintain a positive attitude and a high energy level even when opportunities are scarce, you're going to do better than someone who doesn't even want to get out of bed in the morning.

Good times or bad, the fundamentals of sales remain pretty much the same. And when you've discovered that basic truth, you're a long way toward selling when no one is buying.

Good luck!

Index

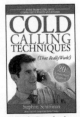

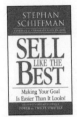
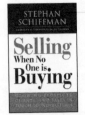

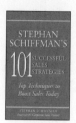

Trade Paperback
$19.95
ISBN 10: 1-59337-376-7
ISBN 13: 978-1-59337-376-4

Trade Paperback
$16.95
ISBN 10: 1-59869-228-3
ISBN 13: 978-1-59869-228-0

Trade Paperback
$10.95
ISBN 10: 1-58062-813-3
ISBN 13: 978-1-58062-813-6

Trade Paperback
$9.95
ISBN 10: 1-59337-273-6
ISBN 13: 978-1-59337-273-6

Schiffman's *25 Sales* Series
Everything they didn't teach you in business school!

Trade Paperback
$7.95
ISBN 10: 1-59869-821-4
ISBN 13: 978-1-59869-821-3

Trade Paperback
$6.95
ISBN 10: 1-59337-014-8
ISBN 13: 978-1-59337-014-5

Trade Paperback
$6.95
ISBN 10: 1-59869-757-9
ISBN 13 : 978-1-59869-757-5

Trade Paperback
$6.95
ISBN 10: 1-58062-614-9
ISBN 13: 978-1-58062-614-9

Trade Paperback
$6.95
ISBN 10: 1-58062-116-3
ISBN 13: 978-1-58062-116-8